i just want you to be happy

Preventing and tackling teenage depression

Professors
Leanne Rowe,
David Bennett
and **Bruce Tonge**

ALLEN&UNWIN

The information in this book is based on the research and personal and professional experiences of the authors. It is not intended as a substitute for consulting with your doctor or other health professional. The names of the people described in this book have been changed to protect their privacy. The authors have not received any remuneration or benefit from the pharmaceutical industry.

Proceeds will be donated towards further research into the mental health and wellbeing of children and young people.

First published in 2009

Copyright © David Bennett and Anne Bennett,
Acacia Arch Pty Ltd and Bruce Tonge 2009

Allen & Unwin
83 Alexander Street
Crows Nest NSW 2065
Australia
Phone: (61 2) 8425 0100
Fax: (61 2) 9906 2218
Email: info@allenandunwin.com
Web: www.allenandunwin.com

National Library of Australia
Cataloguing-in-Publication entry:

Rowe, Leanne.
I just want you to be happy / Leanne Rowe, David Bennett, Bruce Tonge.

ISBN: 978 1 74175 530 5 (pbk.)

Includes index.
Bibliography.

Depression in adolescence–Australia–Prevention.
Depression, Mental–Treatment–Australia.
Teenagers–Mental health–Australia.
Bennett, David, 1944-
Tonge, Bruce J. (Bruce John)

616.852700835

Internal photographs: bigstockphoto.com and stock.xchang
Set in 10.5/15 pt Electra LH by Bookhouse, Sydney
Printed in Australia by McPherson's Printing Group

10 9 8 7 6 5 4 3 2

In memory of our dedicated colleague,
Dr Khulod Maarouf-Hassan, who was
tragically killed by a young patient in her
general practice on 16 June 2006

Acknowledgements

The authors wish to acknowledge the following people who believed in this book and provided constructive feedback throughout its development:

Dr Chris Mitchell, Ms Leonie Young, Professor Brett McDermott, Dr Brian Graetz, Associate Professor Michael Baigent, Ms Julie Foster, Mr Mark Rosser, Ms Teri Snowden, Ms Jennifer Faulkner, Dr Stewart Birt, members of the RACGP National Standing Committee Quality, Ms Amanda Dudley, Dr Glenn Melvin, Dr Avril Brereton, Mrs Anne Bennett, Dr Peter Jasek.

We also greatly appreciate the dedicated work of Allen & Unwin staff including Annette Barlow, Catherine Milne, Siobhán Cantrill, and freelancer Elizabeth Keenan, who nurtured this book and its authors.

Authors

Associate Professor Leanne Rowe AM MBBS, DipRACOG, FRACGP, FAICD, MD, is a general practitioner who runs a medical practice for medical practitioners in Melbourne and is deputy chancellor of Monash University. She currently serves on the boards of Medibank Private and *beyondblue: the national depression initiative*. In the past, she was chairman of the Royal Australian College of General Practitioners (RACGP) and the director of Clockwork Young People's Health Service for disadvantaged youth. She was recently awarded a doctor of medicine degree on the topic of youth depression and the Rose Hunt Medal for service to medicine by the RACGP.

Clinical Professor David Bennett AO MBBS, FRACP, FSAM is an adolescent health physician involved in wide-ranging efforts to improve the health and well-being of young people. He is head of NSW Centre for the Advancement of Adolescent Health at The Children's Hospital at Westmead, national president of the Association for the Wellbeing of Children in Healthcare and chairman of the board of management of Ku-ring-gai Youth Development Service in Sydney. David was honoured with an AO for 'service to medicine, particularly in the field of adolescent health and medical care', and named a Paul Harris Fellow with Rotary International for service to the community.

Professor Bruce Tonge, MD, DPM, MRCPsych, FRANZCP is head of the Monash University School of Psychology, Psychiatry and Psychological Medicine and the Centre for Developmental Psychology and Psychiatry and also the senior adviser to Southern Health Child and Adolescent Mental Health Service. He is an

experienced child and adolescent psychiatrist who is recognised
internationally for his extensive research publication and teaching
on mental health problems in children and adolescents, including
the assessment, phenomenology and treatment of anxiety and
depression. He is also a member of the Boards of the Mental
Health Foundation of Australia, Resilience Australia, Neuroscience
Victoria and Neuroscience Australia and chairs the Board of Autism
Victoria.

Foreword

by *beyondblue: the national depression initiative*

As I travel around Australia and talk with parents, teachers and carers about *beyondblue*'s work with young people, I see similarities in the need for accurate and timely information regarding depression for parents and young people—about the signs, symptoms and where to get help.

Since its inception in 2000, the wellbeing of young Australians has been *beyondblue*'s priority. This is reflected in our growing range of resources produced specifically for young people, the proliferation of our awareness-raising activities, new research programs and Youthbeyondblue's involvement in national youth activities.

beyondblue is taking a leading role in providing this information, not only to parents—but also to mental health professionals—to improve the outcomes for young people affected by depression.

To help achieve this, we have formed a committee of mental health experts who are working closely with the National Health and Medical Research Council to produce a new set of clinical guidelines for health professionals who work with young people.

I am proud to endorse this book, which I consider to be a great addition to the literature on depression and which will be of assistance to parents and young people throughout Australia.

The Hon. Jeff Kennett AC
Chairman
beyondblue: the national depression initiative

Foreword
by The Royal Australian College of General Practitioners

Teenage years are a time of exploration and discovery and, for some, finding their own path on this journey can be challenging. There are many factors that impact on the mental health of young people, including their relationships with friends at school, with their teachers and with their family; their economic situation; their cultural background; and the progress of their education.

We all want to think that our kids are perfect or that they won't experience conditions like depression. But part of being an adult carer, parent or health worker means facing the facts and not putting our head in the sand. Fortunately depression can be prevented and managed. The valuable resources and advice covered in this book may be able to help members of your family or young people whom you know to meet their personal challenges before depression comes on and to work through depression if it arrives.

As parents, friends, relatives and as doctors we want to provide a supportive, safe and reassuring environment in which the teenagers we know and care for can embark on this journey confident that they have support mechanisms in place, should they need to access them.

I strongly support the proactive, healthy approach to preventing and managing depression as outlined in this important book. The authors have put together a well-researched, accessible resource that provides practical advice to boost the resilience of families facing the challenge of teenage depression.

Dr Chris Mitchell
President
The Royal Australian College of General Practitioners

Contents

Introduction

A lifetime of happiness...would be hell on earth.
—George Bernard Shaw

At a time when parents just want their children to be happy, depression among young Australians is increasing. It is a serious problem for young people, their families and society.

No one is immune. Status, wealth, and health are no defence. Whatever their background, teenagers live in an age of social and global change, violent and sexual media images, high levels of family breakdown, and disconnected communities. As well as depression, young people increasingly fall prey to bullying, eating disorders, drug and alcohol abuse, unwanted pregnancy and homelessness. But our work with thousands of families over many years has left us optimistic that many of these problems can be prevented or solved: lives can be healed.

As doctors, we have become frustrated with the 'head in the sand' approach to caring for depressed young people. There is plenty of evidence, for example, that certain parenting styles can protect against depression. Yet many parents think parenting courses and books are for other people—the people who really have problems. 'It won't happen in our family,' they tell us. 'There's no training for the most important job in the world.' 'Our teenagers are OK,' they'll say, 'so we don't have to worry about depression.' 'There's nothing I can do to influence my teenagers—they are more influenced by friends, school and the media.' 'It's normal for teenagers to be moody and grumpy.' 'My kids are in their late teens, so it's too late anyway.' Or, 'It's all too hard, I haven't got time.' Conversely expectations for their teenagers to be constantly happy are very counter-productive.

Contrary to popular myth, depression in young people can be prevented, or picked up early and treated effectively. This book brings together not only sound, well-supported information on the topic but also our combined experience of working with young people (and their families) who are stressed or otherwise in trouble.

It also provides parents, as well as teachers and other caring adults with a guide to resources that can help with parenting and mental health problems. These resources include general practitioners, who can give information and advice on depression in routine consultations.

This book covers:

- How to prevent youth depression
- How to recognise and treat depression early
- The difference between normal sadness and depression
- The warm, respectful parenting style that helps protect young people from depression
- How to resolve common conflicts between parents and teenagers
- How to promote a healthy lifestyle
- Facing up to bullying
- How to teach young people to think optimistically and manage stress
- How to make school a plus, not a problem
- How to respond in a crisis and where to get the right help

I Just Want You to Be Happy is a call to action to parents, grand-parents, other extended family, teachers, health and welfare professionals and all adults who care about young people. It's time to change the future for young Australians.

Leanne Rowe, David Bennett, Bruce Tonge

Part 1

What is the problem?

Young people need just one good parent, one good teacher and one good friend.

Depression among young people is a serious and growing problem in Australia. One in five teenagers will experience depression before the age of eighteen. In just one year, many hundreds of thousands of prescriptions for antidepressants are written for Australians under eighteen. Depressed teenagers become depressed adults, and anxiety and depression are the most common health problem in women and the third most common in men. But statistics aren't needed to convince anyone of the importance of this issue. Most Australians know from first-hand experience how depression wrecks lives, particularly when it affects children.

Young people become depressed for many reasons. They may reach puberty before their schoolmates do. They may be bullied or feel left out. They may have a parent who is violent or depressed. They may seek escape in alcohol and other drugs, particularly cannabis, only to be plunged into depression instead. It is difficult for parents to exclude such risks entirely from their children's lives. Our materialistic society doesn't help. It encourages us to seek endless euphoria through buying new things and having new experiences, but it leaves many of us in a permanent state of dissatisfaction.

Let's start by looking at depression — and how it differs from normal teenager sadness and grumpiness.

1
What is normal teenage behaviour?

There are times when parenthood seems nothing but feeding the mouth that bites you.
—Peter De Vries, *The Tunnel of Love*

L iving with an adolescent has been likened to riding an emotional roller-coaster. A seemingly happy and confident kid can suddenly lash out angrily, become painfully self-conscious or turn blackly pessimistic. Most parents understand that growing up can be difficult—they went through it themselves. What's important to know is where an ordinary down period ends and depression begins.

Even before the earliest signs of puberty appear, children experience emotional shifts as their internal chemistry starts to change. Without knowing quite how or why, they start to feel different, awkward, unsettled. As puberty progresses, they get moody and emotionally volatile. Hormones are often blamed. Rapidly rising levels of testosterone give boys a marked increase in sex drive, energy and a need to move. Surging oestrogen levels can make girls weepy, emotional—and almost desperate to communicate. For both sexes, the teenage years are a time of extreme sensitivity. Particularly in the early stages, anything—or nothing at all—can touch off a mood swing.

Bursts of euphoria are as common as episodes of gloom. A recently miserable teenager might start giggling at something that to an adult seems patently unfunny. Sudden exuberant shouts after hours of quiet absorption in a computer game, or endless yakking on the phone about a new love affair, are good signs: this is what normal adolescence looks and sounds like.

Adolescence is the time when we work out who we are, what we believe, what is our cultural and religious identity, what we are good or not so good at, and what interests us. During that long and often painful process, teenagers copy the clothing, attitudes and behaviour of people they like or admire. They define their own style through choices in music, sport or hobbies. This is also a time when teenagers develop and 'practise' their sexuality through fantasy, observation of others and tentative, then more passionate, relationships.

Time out to refurbish emotionally

During these years, kids need time to be alone. They need time out to ponder momentous questions like, 'Am I normal?' 'Who am I?' 'Who will I become?' 'What should I believe in?' They may retreat physically, to the bedroom or some other private place, or just become withdrawn and unwilling to talk. Silence provides a sort of psychological privacy. 'Absolutely nothing happened at school today' is a way of saying 'I want to keep my thoughts to myself.' Psychologists call this process 'introspective withdrawal' and consider it extremely important. One group of researchers used long-range beepers to track what teenagers were doing and how they were feeling at different points in the day. They found that young people are often melancholy when they're alone but that after a while their mood lightens, as if they've been emotionally refurbished by solitude.

But where do emotional ups and downs stop being normal? How can we tell when the way kids are acting is something to worry about?

Adolescent thinking and the brain

We now know a lot more about some aspects of adolescent behaviour thanks to recent studies that used magnetic resonance imaging (MRI) to take snapshots of children's brains at two-year intervals. Some areas of the human brain are mature by the end of childhood. These areas don't change any further. But the prefrontal cortex—responsible for controlling impulses and emotions and anticipating the likely consequences of one's actions—is not yet mature. This area continues to develop through the teenage years. The highest-level areas of the prefrontal cortex may not be completely mature until people hit their twenties.

Teenage brains, in other words, are not yet fully adult. They are changing in a way that makes their owners more open to new ideas and change but also more likely to experiment and take risks. An immature brain plus a flood of hormones, especially in the case of boys, where testosterone promotes thrill-seeking and limit-testing, is a potentially dangerous mix.

The prefrontal cortex has been called the 'area of sober second thought' because when it is mature it helps us reason better, develop more self control and make better judgements. This is a helpful—and hopeful—point for parents who may be struggling with a teenager's erratic and otherwise infuriatingly normal behaviour.

Adolescent daydreaming

Many parents and teachers recognise that intellectual and emotional development take time, but it's easy to lose patience when teenagers seem completely oblivious to us. As one teacher commented in a school report, 'Jack spends a lot of time contemplating matters other than those immediately to hand.' As one girl put it: 'Parents and teachers don't have a clue what goes on in our heads.' Fortunately, daydreaming too is part of normal development.

Adolescent daydreams are complex. They may be disjointed and vague, romantic or heroic, sinister or vicious. They are important to the dreamers, but rarely shared with adults. There are good reasons for this. Daydreaming lets adolescents try out different behaviours in their imaginations without having to face the hazards of the real world. This is especially true of erotic fantasies. It lets kids privately plan ahead and thus gain motivation and confidence. Daydreaming—as adults too know—also provides a temporary escape from the stresses of everyday life. Persistent vague and inattentive behaviour can, however, indicate a hearing or learning problem, especially in boys. It may also be a sign that a teenager is worried or stressed. Asking the teenager if anything is troubling them might help decide if things need to be taken further.

So what's a parent to do?

Giving in to frustration and tearing out your hair may be one way to go, but possibly not the most effective one. Seeking an instant explanation doesn't always work, either—you are liable to be told, 'Leave me alone, stop bugging me.'

Perhaps the best approach is to ask if there's a problem without expecting an answer right away, and be ready to engage when the teenager is ready to talk. Despite appearances to the contrary, adolescents are continually seeking their parents' love and approval. When they don't get it, they may behave as if they have given up and start needling and being annoying. Paradoxically, ignoring a parent can be one of the most effective ways of getting his or her attention!

That's the other important thing parents can do: pay attention. If we can stand by and listen without becoming uptight, over-anxious or overcontrolling, be sympathetic but calm, and go easy on the advice, the situation can remain manageable. The key is to convey that we endorse the child and have faith in him or her. We also need to bear in mind that relationships between parents and teenagers cannot always be sunny, no matter how much we might want them to be. Tempests and troubles are a normal part of healthy relationships. But paying attention helps us pick up the signs of a real problem.

The messages to remember

- Adolescence is a time of rapid change and exuberance, but also of emotional upheaval, moodiness and erratic behaviour.

- Highs and lows are part of life, and all teenagers must learn how to deal with them in order to become strong, mature adults.

- The prefrontal cortex, aptly described as the 'area of sober second thought', matures late. This helps explain the impulsive, risky behaviour typical of adolescence.

- Persistent sadness, grumpiness or irritability may signal depression and should be acted on.

- The starting point for parents is listening. Their actions and comments should convey the idea: 'I believe in you. You are going to be OK.'

2
Is it sadness or depression?

Happiness comes of the capacity to feel deeply, to
enjoy simply, to think freely…and to be needed.
—Margaret Storm Jameson

During the ups and downs of adolescence, many parents
will ask the question: 'Is this behaviour something to
worry about?' Emotional lows are, as we've seen, quite
normal, and even the everyday kind—when the cat dies or an exam
is failed—call for sympathy. Parents are usually able to recognise
reactions to specific stressful events, and few would underestimate
the suffering involved. At such times, comfort and support are all
that is needed.

But most parents are also aware that depression is common and
know what damage it can do to lives and relationships. So what are
the signs that a teenager has moved beyond being down in the dumps
or sad to having depression? Not all teenagers react to depression in
the same way, but these are some general indicators:

**Depressed young people are persistently sad and down-
hearted.** When a painful or stressful event is over, they don't bounce
back. They want to pick themselves up but can't. If a teenager
remains tearful, sullen and out of sorts for two weeks or more, it's

a sign something is amiss. Depressed adolescents appear to lose interest in life and take little pleasure in activities they used to enjoy. They become apathetic and have trouble thinking and concentrating—deteriorating school work is a dead giveaway. They pull away from other people, including family and friends. They may spend a lot more time in their room or glued to the computer. They may medicate themselves with alcohol, cannabis or other drugs. When parents start to feel sad vibes coming through most of the time and think, 'I don't know you any more', there's likely to be more going on than an ordinary bout of the sads.

Depressed young people are often physically unwell. They may complain of frequent headaches, other aches and pains or the general 'blahs'. Excessive tiredness and lack of energy are also very common. They may spend half the night tossing and turning or lying awake, unable to get back to sleep. They may sleep during the day and stay up at night; this can be a way of isolating themselves. They may eat more—or stop eating—and either gain or lose a lot of weight. Arguments with parents over missed meals may make young people withdraw even more. Depression can also result from ill-health. Viral infections such as glandular fever can leave teenagers feeling fatigued for months and may trigger a persisting depression. Drinking alcohol and smoking cannabis can lead to depression, which in turn may lead to more drinking and drug abuse.

Depressed young people may behave in ways that are unusual for them. One of the clearest signs of teenage depression is persistent irritability—fierce and uncharacteristic. Everything seems to be too much trouble, 'everyone is stupid', and trivial things can trigger angry outbursts. The shouting and snapping and door-slamming may not *look* like depression, but the sadness will be evident if you look and listen carefully. Kids with a history of being somewhat hyperactive and naughty may become even more disruptive, impulsive, aggressive or frankly antisocial (for example, stealing). This may get them into trouble with the police. Instead of treatment for their depression, they receive punishment at the hands of the authorities (school, welfare agencies or the courts). It is unlikely to help and may make their depression worse.

In more severe forms of depression, teenagers have unrelentingly gloomy thoughts, feelings of anguish, loss and hopelessness, and a mounting sense of frustration or fear. Their very existence becomes painful, and the idea of escape through suicide becomes deeply appealing. They may think about death. They may contemplate suicide. Some feel life is empty and futile. As one girl said: 'When you're really depressed you think, "What is the point?" You live, accomplish nothing and then die.' Some decide they are so useless that they deserve to die. If they've clashed with a friend or parent, they may think that if they themselves were dead it would fix the problem. Or they may conceive of suicide as a way to get back at those who have hurt them. In these cases the young person may not fully understand that death is final. She may vaguely expect that somehow, magically, suicide will solve all problems and she will return to a better life.

Hopefully, before this advanced stage is reached, someone will have tuned into what is going on. Studies of teenage suicides show that in the month before their death, most mentioned their despair to someone—if not a parent, then a teacher, GP or friend. Paying attention, in such cases, can be a matter of life and death. If the alarm is sounded, professional help sought and the right support provided, teenage suicides can be prevented.

Lucy

It is her fourth cold in three months. She is chronically tired and has stomach pains, which are preventing her from going to school. Lucy is a shy, sensitive fifteen-year-old. Her parents have taken her to naturopaths, chiropractors, then the family GP, who referred her to a psychologist. The consultation with the psychologist went like this: 'I sense that something else is wrong.' 'No.' 'Are you worried about anything?' 'No.' 'How is school?' 'Good.' 'Who do you hang around with at school?' 'Nobody.' Then, with tears welling in her eyes, Lucy said: 'My friends have dumped me. They swear at me. Older kids stole my bag. No one cares and everything is my fault. I'm bored and I've got nothing to do.'

Is Lucy being bullied or is she depressed, or both?

A diagnosis of depression is made if a teenager has had **continously, for two weeks or more, either**:

• Depressed and/or irritable mood

or

• Decreased interest in activities

and five of the following symptoms:

• Change in appetite and significant gain in weight, or loss, or failure to gain weight as expected
• Sleeping difficulties
• Physical agitation
• Fatigue or loss of energy
• Feelings of worthlessness
• Decreased ability to think clearly
• Thoughts of death

The kinds of questions to ask Lucy are: 'How long have you been feeling sad? When can you last remember feeling happy? How has your school work been going? What are your usual interests and have you been interested in them lately? How are your friendships? How is your appetite? Have you lost or gained weight recently? How are you sleeping? If the bullying stopped, would you feel completely better? Would that fix everything?'

If Lucy says she's felt sad or uninterested in her usual activities for over two weeks in a row, it is likely that she is depressed and requires treatment. On the other hand, if her problems resolve when her teachers intervene and stop the bullying, we would generally conclude that she is not depressed, just responding appropriately to a stressful situation. In this case, reassurance and validation may be all that she needs.

Tim

Fourteen-year-old Tim, the middle of three boys, was in Year 8 at high school. His father was an engineer and his mother a management consultant. Tim had always been a sociable, pleasant and happy kid with plenty of friends. Neither his parents nor his teachers were worried about him except that they felt he could do better academically. However, over recent months, they had noticed a change. He had become obnoxious, rude, argumentative, both at home and at school and, of course, his room was a mess. Although a good basketball player, he now wanted to drop out of the team and also give up his clarinet lessons.

What could be happening here? Is this behaviour part of normal adolescent rebellion or something to worry about? When this case is presented in forums, unfortunately some parents respond with negative comments such as:

- This is normal fourteen-year old behaviour.
- The other children in the family turned out fine, so it can't be the parents' fault.

- It is his mother's fault because she's working.
- His behaviour is completely inexplicable.

Any sudden change in behaviour is a cause for concern. There is always a reason—absent parents, permissive parenting, parental marital problems, bullying at school, early onset of mental illness. The first questions to ask in this case are: Does Tim think there is a problem? What does he think it is due to? Why? If the behaviour continues or deteriorates, Tim's parents can focus on creating a loving environment at home, looking at ways of overcoming family conflict, visiting the class teacher to discuss school performance, encouraging Tim to invite his friends home to gain an understanding of his relationships with them, and creating a safety net of family, friends, school and community.

Parents can try to focus on what they can do, rather than creating more problems by attempting to control what they cannot control. Young people respond well in the long term to consistency, quiet confidence and perseverance through difficult times.

Carlo

Carlo is fourteen. He was taken to a psychiatrist by his mother at the suggestion of the school counsellor. Eighteen months before, Carlo's father had died suddenly at the age of 40 from a stroke. Carlo, his mother, and his younger brother and sister were all shocked and stricken with grief. But with lots of support from the wider family and community, they gradually recovered—all except Carlo. He became increasingly irritable, angry and uncooperative at home. He stopped playing football and hockey and shunned his friends. He stayed for hours at a time in his room, watching television, or wandered aimlessly in a park near the house. He was negative and pessimistic about himself and his future. In a school essay, he wrote that there was no point to life. This led the school counsellor to refer him for help.

When Carlo walked in, he was clearly resentful. He muttered crossly while his mother explained the background. He didn't seem to want to talk, but agreed to draw a picture of a bad dream. When he drew an angry monster, the psychiatrist asked him to draw what happened next. He drew a picture of himself being attacked by the monster, which he said 'wrecks my brain'. Asked how he felt about that, he said it made him very sad and drew tears on the pictured Carlo's face.

What did Carlo know about the cause of his father's tragic death, we asked. 'His brain was wrecked by a stroke.' Could the monster Carlo had drawn be the one that wrecked his father's brain? Could Carlo draw a picture of that happening? He added a picture of his father's dismembered head shooting above his own. How did Carlo feel about the monster and his father's death? 'Really angry.' What would he like to do to the monster that had caused his father's death? 'Kill it,' he said, and drew a picture of himself shooting the monster and bullets going into its head. As well as feeling sad, was he also angry with his father for dying? Yes, Carlo said, but he felt angrier with himself.

By now Carlo was talking freely. He said that a short time before his father died they'd had an argument. His father had asked him to mow the lawn. Carlo refused, and went out with his mates. The argument made his father late for golf, and he set off angrily through the nearby park, headed for the golf course. He never got there. The park where he died was the same park where Carlo had taken to wandering aimlessly. Clearly, he blamed himself for his father's death. Asked who he thought the monster really was, he said, 'Me, I'm the monster.' This made him feel '100 per cent sad and bad', he added. He thought he'd be better off dead himself.

However, with psychological treatment and support from his mother and teachers, Carlo recovered.

Carlo's story shows how the normal process of grieving over the death of a loved one can trigger a depressive illness.

The messages to remember

- Not all teenagers who are sad, morose or miserable are depressed. Such reactions can be appropriate responses to life's ups and downs.

- Depression should be suspected if a teenager who is sad, downhearted, withdrawn, uncharacteristically irritable or vaguely unwell remains in that state for more than two weeks.

- If depression is suspected, getting the right help is important. The condition *can* be successfully treated, but if it is not picked up and treated, the consequences can be grave.

3
What makes young people vulnerable—or resilient?

Resilience is the happy knack of being able to bungy jump through the pitfalls of life.
—Andrew Fuller

Because distressing situations make most people unhappy, it is easy to conclude that depressed adolescents must be living in distressing circumstances—that they must be orphans or very poor, or have parents who are divorced, ill, drunk or abusive. But depression often occurs in young people from seemingly happy, well-adjusted families. How can that be?

There are many theories about why young people become depressed. We know that depression is more likely to hit teenagers who have a poorly developed sense of identity or who feel powerless to change their circumstances. Bad life experiences, unusual sensitivity and high-achieving personalities also put young people at risk. Unrealistic parental expectations and excessive parental control or criticism can also tip the balance towards depression. So can the materialism and shallow individualism of modern society.

Our misguided cultural values

'The 20th century, for all its scientific and technological amazements...was a century in which we watered down our own humanity—turning wisdom into information, community into consumerism, politics into manipulation, destiny into DNA—making it increasingly difficult to find nourishment for the hungers of the heart.'

—P.J. Palmer in the Foreword to Kessler, R., *The Soul of Education—Helping Students Find A Connection, Compassion and Character at School*, ASCD, Baltimore, 2000.

The social researcher Hugh Mackay, in his book *Advance Australia...Where?* (2007), looks at the so-called Generation Y (people born between 1978 and 1994). He calls them the options generation, and says they are flexible, open to change, cooperative—and the most tribal generation we have seen: 'They are world champions at establishing intimate, supportive relationships with their peers, standing by each other, and staying connected.' These qualities are healthy and protective. And they are all the more needed in our individualistic, materialistic, consumption-driven society.

There is convincing evidence that when we seek happiness in the pursuit of money and material possessions we are all too likely to end up dissatisfied, anxious, angry, isolated, alienated and depressed. Richard Eckersley discusses this at length in his thought-provoking book *Well & Good—Happiness, Morality and Meaning (2004)*.

Individualism, too, has a downside. An excess of freedom and choice can lead to a heightened sense of risk, uncertainty and insecurity, and a sense that we alone are to blame if we fail or miss out. The American psychologist Martin Seligman has linked increasing individualism to the

rising incidence of depression. The tribalism Mackay notes
among young people may be a very human response to the
isolation that individualism can bring. It is no accident,
Eckersley suggests, that the most popular drugs today are
those—alcohol, marijuana and party drugs such as ecstasy—
that dissolve the boundaries of the self and induce a sense
of merging with others.

Another questionable social value is our obsession
with celebrity. People who make fame and glamour their
goals—who get validation from others, not from within, also
tend to be more anxious and depressed and less trusting
and caring in their relationships than people oriented towards
close relationships, personal growth and self-understanding,
and contributing to the community. Seligman argues that
healthy individuals—and a healthy society—strike a balance
between commitment to the self and commitment to the
common good.

Who is most at risk?

Some young people are more vulnerable to stress than their peers,
especially those who have low self-esteem and feel left out and
unloved. These teenagers lack the resilience that helps other kids
cope reasonably well even with great trials and troubles, and it's
they who are more likely to have emotional problems such as
depression. Special attention should be given to:

Young people who are different. Feeling different can be
painful for adolescents, who need to fit in so as to feel worthwhile
and respected. Those with a chronic illness or disability, those
confused about their sexual orientation, and those from racial,
religious or ethnic minorities may have particular difficulty finding
their place, and this can put them at greater risk of depression.

Young people who experience trauma or personal loss. It's understandable that losing a parent through death or separation; being rejected by a parent; having parents who are alcoholic or suffer from chronic or mental illness; or experiencing abuse can lead to depression. For reasons that are unclear, the death of a father during earlier childhood can increase the risk of depression in the teen years. This may suggest that fathers play an important role in building confidence and self-esteem.

Young people in stressful or deprived circumstances. Being homeless, unemployed or very poor, being an immigrant or refugee, or living in institutional care or even in remote areas can all increase a teenager's risk of depression.

Girls. Girls are twice as likely to experience depression as boys. This may be because they go through puberty earlier, with the associated rush of female hormones and mood swings. It may result from a difference in the way girls think about feelings and emotions. Or perhaps girls are more likely to experience domestic violence and sexual abuse, with the resulting feelings of violation and helplessness.

Gay and lesbian teenagers. A big part of growing up is coming to know who one is sexually. Gay adolescents feel different, and many struggle alone with uncertainty, confusion and fear. They often have low self-worth, lose friends, and are verbally and physically abused by their peers. They are two to three times more likely than straight peers to become depressed or to attempt suicide. They are usually reluctant to come out, especially to their parents. Fears of parental disapproval are not always unfounded, so it can come as an enormous relief to meet other gay people and share concerns and experiences.

Identifying teenagers who are vulnerable to or showing early signs of depression, is important. But as parents and care-givers, we can do much to help immunise adolescents against depressive illness.

Resilience and how to build it

'All kids need is a little help, a little hope, and somebody who believes in them'. In this insightful remark, basketball star Earvin 'Magic' Johnson more or less sums up the building blocks of resilience.

Resilience comes from the Latin word *resilere*, which means 'to spring or bounce back'. It's been defined as the innate human ability to rebound from adversity with even greater strength to meet future challenges and the potential to achieve positive life outcomes in spite of risk. As the American psychologist Lynne Michael Blum puts it: 'Building resilience is a never-ending upward spiral of coping with and taking charge of problems, solving them one at a time, and transforming failures into strategies that can be used to cope with and take charge of the next problem.'[1] Resilience, in other words, helps us overcome challenges. And overcoming challenges helps us develop greater resilience. Resilience makes young people better able to cope with what life throws at them. Studies that have followed children through adolescence and into adulthood find that no matter what challenges and difficulties they confront, about 60 per cent emerge on the other side as stable, effective and optimistic people.

To some extent, resilience depends on inner strengths: intelligence, social skills, responsibility, motivation. But we shouldn't assume that if children are not born with resilience they will never have it. Resilience also depends on external supports, such as a warm and well-functioning family, positive influence from peers, caring teachers, and a supportive school environment. By helping to provide those supports, adults can help young people build resilience. With the right care and support, even children who have been through severe trauma can turn their lives around.

All children encounter negative situations and stresses, which we call risk factors. Most children also have positive factors in their lives: things that help to protect them from stresses and their consequences. In life there is a constant interplay between protective factors such as family support, physical health, coping skills, literacy and risk factors such as lack of family support, drug use, poor coping skills, learning problems. The more protective factors can be put in place in young people's lives, the more resilient they are likely to become. If risk factors predominate, however, resiliency is far less likely to develop.

For young people, the most powerful protective factor is the presence in their life of a single caring adult. Father Chris Riley, director of the Youth Off the Streets program, based in Sydney, passionately believes this. 'Each of us has the capacity to become that one caring adult in an at-risk child's life,' he says, 'that most potent protective factor that helps hold risk at bay.' Riley sees every young person, no matter how damaged or difficult, as potentially resilient. He refuses to see any teenager as a hopeless case or a lost cause. He has high expectations of those who enter his program—and he is rarely disappointed. 'When we have done a good job as caregivers,' he says, 'the youth we care for can become caregivers themselves.'

There is a surprising consensus about the elements of resilience in young people, though different people sum up these elements in different ways. An inspiring American Indian organisation called the Circle of Courage says that resilience is built by satisfying four basic needs:

- **To satisfy the need for belonging, build trust**
- **To satisfy the need for mastery, recognise talent**
- **To satisfy the need for independence, promote power**
- **To satisfy the need for generosity, instil purpose**

A study of hundreds of thousands of children and youth across North America identified 40 factors—half of them internal and half external—that build resilience and help children grow into healthy adults. These can be boiled down into five Cs: connection, competence, confidence, character and contribution. A resilient person can form social bonds, solve problems and bring plans to fruition, exercise self-control and adhere to principles, and help others.

Some people say that self-esteem makes young people resilient. While self-esteem can be beneficial, it is not enough on its own. As Richard Eckersley points out in *Well and Good*: 'People with high self-esteem can be obnoxious, narcissistic, aggressive, disparaging and inclined to take excessive risks . . . self-control is worth ten times as much as self-esteem.' (See Bibliography)

Other researchers have concluded that resilient children can form close relationships, can trust others, have a sense of autonomy and independence, can solve problems, can persevere in the face of difficulty, and have a sense of purpose or belief that gives meaning to their life.

So while the various definitions of resilience are worded differently, there is a broad consensus on what resilience involves. The point is not to tick every box on every list. The important thing, says English psychiatrist Michael Rutter, is that young people should be enabled to 'approach life's challenges with a positive frame of mind, a confidence that one can deal with the situation, and a repertoire of approaches that are well adapted to one's own personal style of doing things.'

Parents can do much to build that positive approach. Next, we'll look at how differing parenting styles can nurture—or stifle— resilience.

The messages to remember

- Even teenagers from happy, stable homes may have depression. No one is immune. While the causes of depression among young people are varied and sometimes complex, parents, teachers and other caring adults can do much to help.

- Some characteristics of modern society worsen the stresses of adolescence and may contribute to anxiety and depression.

- We should pay careful attention to teenagers who seem unusually sad or upset, especially those in high-risk groups.

- Resilience is a quality that helps us bounce back from difficulties and setbacks.

- Adults can help build resilience in young people by giving them support, care and a warm environment— family, school and community.

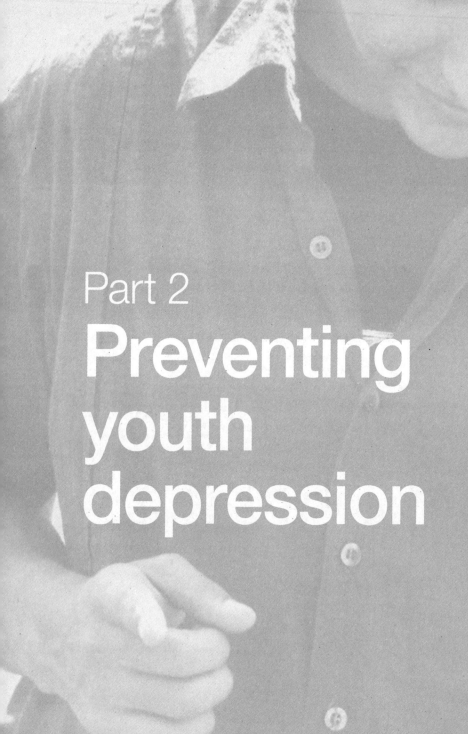

Part 2
Preventing youth depression

Spontaneity and curiosity are the building blocks of good mental health

Spontaneity and curiosity are the building blocks of good mental health ... If you want to teach your children how to have good mental health and how to lead a life that is fulfilling and joyful, you need to show them. They need to see you having fun, being spontaneous, and making mistakes and getting over them. If you want your kids to succeed you need to show them that success is worth having.

—Fuller, A. *Raising Real People: Creating a resilient family*, ACER Press, Melbourne, 2000, p. 28

As parents, we have more influence than we think we do. A good parenting style can be one of the best ways of protecting children from depression. We can divide parenting styles into four broad types.

Parents, from warm to cold

We call the most effective style of parenting warm and respectful. Parents who take this approach are loving, nurturing and flexible as appropriate to the child's stage of life, while setting firm rules on important matters such as safety and good behaviour. In this caring but firm approach, sometimes termed 'authoritative parenting', parents encourage the child to make good choices, negotiate conflict constructively, including teaching them how to resolve conflicts with others, and care strongly about personal values. Warm and respectful parents listen and reassure, but they also make it clear when they disagree and why. They exercise control but are flexible enough to adapt that control to their child's level of maturity.

Pressure cooker parents are controlling, but in a rigid, overly restrictive way. Fearing loss of control, they interfere constantly in issues that, in the overall scheme of things, are unimportant: what their child should eat, drink, wear, study and do with her leisure time, who her friends should be and what to aim for. Pressure cooker parents tend to believe incorrectly that mollycoddling a child will prevent them growing into a successful, independent adult. They are emotionally distant, often giving a child advice before they've heard him out—or else not listening at all. When conflict arises they either suppress it or make it worse. They tend to believe that if they lose the small battles on the home front they will lose total control. This parenting approach, sometimes called 'authoritarian parenting', is big on discipline and punishment, generally of the 'Do as I say, not as I do' variety, and is inconsistent in setting and applying rules.

Pressure cooker parenting often makes children withdraw in quiet resentment or display behavioural problems. They find it very difficult to develop a sense of autonomy or gain the important feeling that they have some control over their life. It is the pressure cooker parent who inadvertently puts their child most at risk of depression.

With the 'anything goes' parent, there's hardly any control. Anything goes parents are not only permissive, they also often use material rewards to try to keep their children in a constant state of happiness, which would be better termed transient excitement than true happiness. Their overly relaxed parenting style tends to produce insecure children with poor social skills. Without clear rules and boundaries to test against, adolescents tend to seek their role models and guidance elsewhere, not always with satisfactory results.

Least controlling of all are uncaring parents. Their approach is detached, neglectful and chaotically inconsistent. They find it easier to give in to a child's demands to keep him happy in the moment than to set healthy, consistent limits that may take time to negotiate and trouble to apply. In this type of family, children are adrift and unsupported, and their mental health is likely to suffer.

Anyone who is a parent will understand how easy it is to lapse into a pressure cooker or anything goes approach, especially if we are rushed, work long hours, are sole parents or lack the support of an extended family. But getting the right balance at home can have great benefits for us and our kids. Above all, it can greatly boost their resiliency.

In this section, we look in detail at the warm and respectful approach and how it helps children; how parents can resolve family conflict and help children deal with stress and stay healthy; and how to ensure that kids' school environment, too, is supportive and nurturing.

4

The difference warm, respectful parenting makes

The most infallible way to make your child miserable is to accustom him to obtain everything he desires.

—Jean Jacques Rousseau

I n our multicultural society, 'normal' covers a wide variety of family lifestyles. But there is broad—and increasingly well-supported—agreement on what we as parents need to do to ensure the best outcomes for our children. We have seen how pressure cooker, anything goes and uncaring parents can actually damage children. In this chapter, we look more closely at what 'warm and respectful' parenting involves, and the enormous benefits of showing love, fostering mutual respect and setting limits.

Love, space, understanding
Asked to describe good parents, teenagers generally say that they: love and respect you; give you space when you need it; support your decisions; offer advice only when asked; understand your feelings, needs and problems; and respond to you when you ask for help. This is confirmed by popular wisdom and by extensive research into family dynamics and child psychology.

Warm and respectful parents are:

- Nurturing. They are involved in a loving way in their child's life. This makes the child more responsive to parental influence. It also creates a secure sense of self and a kind inner voice that enable the child to socialise effectively and withstand stress.
- Firm. Warm and respectful parents give predictable support but also set clear limits. This helps build self-discipline by allowing the child to function as a responsible, competent individual, reducing her exposure to risk and protecting her from damaging experiences.
- Autonomy-granting. Warm and respectful parents sort out rights and responsibilities with their child at appropriate stages from childhood through adolescence. This allows for a healthy independence while fostering connections with peers and the wider community.

Sometimes people confuse autonomy (the ability to act according to our own values and beliefs) and independence (not being reliant upon or influenced by others). Warm and respectful parenting encourages the former. Autonomy builds inner confidence while ensuring that children have a sense of connectedness to family and other caring adults. We like to describe this outcome as *healthy independence.*

Love and respect are threads that weave a family together. Studies have confirmed what we intuitively know: teenagers' most important needs are to feel loved and respected by their parents. What helps teenagers feel loved? Here are some of the things they say:

When I look back on my school years, the most important thing that helped was that my mum really listened to me. I just wanted her to understand but not to worry or overreact or do anything or give me advice. She would sometimes stop the car and give me her full attention or stay up late with me just talking on my bed. Most of all she would listen with her kind eyes. She didn't even have to tell me. I knew when she did this that she really loved me.

My parents show me that they love me by sharing the disappointments and the successes. Small comforts mean a lot. Holding someone rather than talking.

Whatever happens during the day, our family has dinner together and we enjoy talking about the day and make plans for the week. Just asking how my day was is enough proof that they care. Sometimes I know that my parents have a lot of worries, but they try to make dinnertime a time that we enjoy together. If there are problems, we talk about them too, but they usually spend time with one of us later. Sometimes Mum gives me a back massage or brings up a hot water bottle at night time. I talk better at night and this helps me to relax.

My parents sometimes go overboard but they always notice when I do something well or I get an award at school or something good happens. My mum has been there through the ups and downs. She gave me a card and it said: 'We are so proud of you and we love you.'

My dad has a great sense of humour and we have fun together. My parents celebrate everything—from the dog's birthday to Anzac Day. We do family activities and this shows that family matters most. Laughter always helps. They aren't religious but they appreciate the wonder of life—they are very spiritual in the way they find meaning in things and take time to talk about the miracle of normal life. It is a very loving family.

My parents have split up. My mum is sometimes hard on me and tells me off. My dad lets me do anything. I want to stay with my mum. She cares about me. Sometimes I go away with Dad on my own. I wish my mum would come but I know she thinks it's best for me to spend some time on my own with Dad. This way I feel closer to him. I know my mum loves me when she lets me do this because I know it hurts her to let me go.

My parents look after each other and spend time just together. I know my parents will not disagree with each other about the rules—they stand together even when I think one of them is disagreeing. Sometimes they drive me crazy but they are really like a solid rock that I can depend on. They love me.

My family could sometimes pay more attention to me, but it's hard for them when there are four other sisters. I still feel loved.

When I am studying, my dad sometimes comes in and puts a hot chocolate on the desk and then leaves without saying anything. It's when he doesn't say anything that he is actually saying he loves me, respects my work and doesn't even ask for anything in return. I love him.

These comments, from interviews given by seventeen- and eighteen-year-olds, describe some of the small things that parents can do to make a difference. Since adolescents constantly seek parental love and approval (even when it's not obvious they're doing so), it is worth thinking about the small, reassuring gestures that can make your teenager feel loved.

Sometimes we unthinkingly put our kids down or signal a lack of consideration. Teenagers talk about how these negative responses make them feel:

My dad gets home late and works every weekend. My mum hates work and takes it out on us and then says: 'I'm doing all this for you.' I feel like saying: 'What exactly are you doing for us?' My parents get up, go to work, get dinner, clean up, get ready for the next day. I feel I should be grateful, but this doesn't feel like it's enough.

My dad yells at me and sometimes slaps me. Then he tells me he loves me when he cools down. He says he loves me, but he doesn't.

I am not as academic as my brother. My parents don't say anything, but I know they love him more than me.

All young people have secret worlds inside them, where they experience intense emotions, confusion and concern about their friends, the world and their future. When they do not receive the reassurance they need, they act as if they have given up, so as to protect themselves from further hurt. When they then try to test their parents by pushing beyond their limits, the real problems begin. At such times it may help to ask: 'Why do you feel you have to test me and try me out? What can I do to help prevent this next time?'

Showing respect

Teenage years are a time of growing self-awareness, a search for identity, curiosity, exploration and experimentation. The challenge is to understand each teenager's individual physical and mental growth and respect her changing needs. Teenagers respect us if we show them respect in meaningful ways. We need to be prepared to change those ways as adolescents change so as to encourage autonomy, initiative and responsibility. We need to give them a sense that we believe in them and are confident they will be able to manage their lives. Here are some comments from teenagers about respect:

> My parents' values don't change. When they set rules, we talk about them. I know when no means no. I have learnt to respect that.

> My parents respect me and this has taught me to be willing to think of others' feelings.

> My parents allow me to totally choose my own path in terms of subjects, relationships—anything. They have learnt to accept that my talents aren't always academic and they have supported me in my crazy ideas and dreams.

> My parents let me have my say, then they offer their views without pushing them onto me.

Dealing with anger and disrespect

Young people can be upset with us at times even when we parent them well. What should we do when they are openly disrespectful and insult or swear at us? We can set an example ourselves by always being civil and courteous. We should also set firm limits regarding insulting language or tone of voice. Calm remarks like these may help:

- **I feel hurt when you use that language or tone.**
- **Why are you angry?**
- **Why are you being disrespectful?**
- **How can we prevent this happening next time we are angry with each other?**

Young people are often disrespectful if they don't feel respected by their parents. Here is what some teenagers have to say:

I hate being compared to other people. My parents say they don't have time for me, but they give time to my brother. And they say things like, 'You got 90 per cent for that exam, what happened to the other 10 per cent?'

My mum says I am just like my older sister. She says, 'I hope you're not becoming like your sister.' It puts me and my sister down. I hate it.

When my mum picks me up from my friends' houses, the first thing she usually says in front of everyone is, 'I hope you behaved yourself. Excuse me, say thank you to Mrs Smith . . .' I feel like hitting her.

'It is better if my parents say, 'I don't agree with that.' But they usually start with, 'Are you stupid? Can't you do anything right?'

Once I told my mum I was not coping and then she told all my friends' mothers. Then my friends asked me if I was coping. It was embarrassing. Mum does not respect me and I don't trust her.

A cool person stands up for things, is individual and thinks for themselves. This is what I am trying to be. My parents want me to conform to their image. We want completely different things and I need my parents to understand this and to respect me.

My mum yells orders at me: 'Dinner's ready, do the dishes, put your washing away.' I don't mind doing these things, but does she have to speak to me like I'm a child?

My dad gives me one-sided lectures about things and he has to be right. He demands that I listen to him and respect him, but when does he plan to start respecting my ideas?

Adolescents are very sensitive to criticism and are easily embarrassed. It is common for them to react by hitting out verbally at their parents. As one teenager said, 'If someone close to you hurts you emotionally, you retaliate, your trust dissolves. You feel alienated. It makes you feel as though you're not normal and you take out your aggression on your family.'

Many teenagers have a strong sense of justice and will admit that unleashing their frustration on innocent bystanders—including parents!—is wrong. It is difficult to be on the receiving end of a barrage of misplaced anger, especially if we are trying to show concern. But rather than retaliating, parents may do better to ask what is behind the anger. What have we said or done? Does it deserve this outburst? Is there something else going on? When we ask these questions, though, we should respect the teenager's privacy. We should also bear in mind that teenagers often misinterpret our concern as interference and lack of trust:

> My parents need to accept that there are times when I don't wish to talk and they shouldn't ask questions. I need my own space, especially when I'm in a bad mood.

> I made a lot of mistakes and my parents keep bringing them up. I feel like I can't make any mistakes without someone jumping at me.

> Parents need to understand that things are different from when they were teenagers. They need to loosen up. For example, my parents often ask if I am coping. This is really negative. If I say I'm not coping, it sounds like I'm inadequate. It would be more positive if they asked me, 'Are you getting enough sleep? Are you OK?' It's just small things like this that make a difference.

We need a balance. Young people need to be given space and to be allowed to develop autonomy. However, if they seem to be in trouble or going astray, it is normal and helpful for parents to show concern. If a teenager is depressed, takes excessive risks or is uncommunicative for prolonged periods, don't just leave her to her own devices. Sometimes it helps to say, 'I respect your need for independence and space, but I love you so much, I need to know you are OK.'

When parents are firm, calm and consistent, teenagers grow to understand their reasoning and respect their feelings in return. One young man observed: 'When I was about thirteen or fourteen, my dad kept saying, "Watch your tone with your mother." I didn't even know what he was talking about. Then, when my brother turned thirteen, I started to notice his tone. I started to say, "Watch your tone with our mother." He would give me one of those looks, but I couldn't stand the way he would grunt at her.'

Over-control

Sometimes parents express their care and concern by being over-controlling. They may try to micromanage every aspect of their child's life—what she eats, wears and even thinks—or impose rigid, repressive rules. If the child doesn't conform, they may criticise and nitpick endlessly. Not surprisingly, this type of parenting rarely works out well. In fact, it can be toxic.

A young person with little room to move finds himself in an extremely stressful situation. He may react in a healthy way, by rebelling and finding a life outside the confines of the family. Or he may seek escape through drugs or other risk-taking behaviour. Some young people just give in and fit into the mould set by parents at the expense of their individual creativity. Older adolescents, in particular, need to have increasing control over their lives and to be respected and treated like adults.

Susan, aged fifteen, arrives home from school to be greeted by her mother with the question, 'Why are you ten minutes late?' When Susan explains that she decided to walk home through the park with her friend Mary, her mother says, 'You never know what predators might be in that park, and you know I don't like that Mary. She doesn't dress properly and gives the wrong sort of message to boys. You know I would prefer you not to see her. Now come and sit down and eat your afternoon tea.'

When Susan says she doesn't feel like eating, her mother says: 'Don't you know that teenagers should eat five nutritious meals a day? Now come and eat it or I won't let you eat again until dinner time. Oh, look, there's a dirty mark on your bottom. Take your uniform off now. I'll have to wash it.' Susan goes to her room, shuts the door and doesn't say the words she wanted to say: 'I actually had a hard day at school, Mum'.

There are three main types of unhealthy parental control:

- **Overprotectiveness. This hinders teenagers' autonomy by shielding them from all potentially challenging or unsafe situations. It breeds anxiety and stifles autonomy. It leaves adolescents no space and no choice, and deprives them of the learning experiences they need to become strong, resilient adults.**
- **Exhausting over-expectation. When parents relentlessly pressure their child to achieve or perform, or be in a constant state of happiness, the child's personal inclinations are suppressed or ignored. This may lead her to feel inadequate or that whatever she does is never good enough. When an adolescent cries, 'I feel like you are pressuring me,' she's not joking. Parents should beware of living vicariously through their children. Having positive expectations of young people**

is important, and no one would question the
desirability of giving them high ideals. But rather than
push them beyond their abilities or shove their personal
interests aside, we should match our expectations with
the likelihood of success—another of those balancing
acts for which we as parents have received no training!

- Bullying. Parents who focus on controlling their
  children by physical punishment like spanking or
  confinement and psychological methods like provoking
  guilt are likely to be met with quiet resentment or
  anger. A bullying approach is one-sided ('You will do it
  because I said so') and counter-productive.
  Paradoxically, it undermines a parent's power and may
  ultimately drive a teenager to reject his parents and
  even leave home. In one of the worst types of
  psychological bullying, a teenager may be made to feel
  responsible for his parent's mental health: 'Don't leave
  me alone again tonight. I don't think I could get
  through another night if you went out again.'

Each type of over-control makes the young person feel powerless
and stuck. She may start to see herself in only negative ways and
become depressed. So why do some parents feel they must control
their children to such a damaging extent? Some are anxious and
under-confident, others find it hard to trust, many are experiencing
marital or mental health problems. Whatever the cause, they focus
their tensions and negative feelings on their child.

Parents have every reason to worry and be concerned for their
children's wellbeing, and it's appropriate for them to set limits
to make sure their children don't get into difficult situations at
a vulnerable age. But clear rules and standards of behaviour are

one thing; over-control is quite another. As parents, we need to continually ask ourselves:

- Am I encouraging my child to grow up to be an autonomous, responsible adult?
- What is the long-term outcome I want for my teenager?

Over-indulgence

Anything goes parents, as we have seen, exercise no control at all. They constantly give in to the demands of teenagers and opt for short-term peace at any price rather than making the best decision for the long term. It's the easy way out. It keeps the child happy for the moment but it does not give her guidance or limits and encourages her to be self-centred. Over-indulgent parents let young people get away with murder. According to one definition, 'Permissiveness is the principle of treating children as if they were adults—and the tactic of making sure they never reach that stage.'

Over-indulgence looks like the opposite of over-control, but it is also a form of holding on. A parental approach that lacks firmness fails to provide a model for an adolescent to either identify with or rebel against, and confusion prevails. While they rarely admit it openly, most children are looking for firmness.

> My dad lets me do anything I like. He doesn't check up if I don't go to school or if I don't come home. But he doesn't care either. My mum's rules drive me crazy and we fight, but she cares.

When limits are not set or are inconsistent and arbitrary, children become unsettled and insecure, and family harmony suffers.

Messages to remember

Good parenting involves:

- showing love and respect

- communicating directly and honestly

- striking a balance between warm intimacy and self-confident autonomy

- showing clear parental authority through responsible decision-making that gives teenagers a say

- negotiating family rules and codes of behaviour within firm limits

- setting a good example in all areas of life

5
Resolving family conflict

Having an argument with a teenager is like being pecked to death by ducks.

—Lawrence Steinberg

Ducks' bills don't really hurt, of course, but an argument with a teenager can be really hurtful and distressing, especially when we're merely trying to do the right thing. Most parents, for example, want to protect their children from harm. But parental protectiveness can seem to teenagers like attempts to fence them in. While young people need firm limits, they often rebel against them, testing their parents' resolve. Maintaining a warm, respectful parenting style in such situations is easier said than done.

Unresolved conflict and lingering resentment are serious, as they can place young people at greater risk of depression. Parents may find it helpful to pick their battles, decide what is important and what can wait or does not really matter. Is the conflict unnecessary? Unwinnable? Can a resolution be negotiated or not? We can learn to respond differently to different types of conflicts, and to avoid overreacting to minor irritations or underreacting in cases where, for example, our child's safety is at risk.

Our normally compliant son has just stormed out of the house shouting, 'You can't make me!' He's right. We can't make him do anything. But adolescents who understand that limits are about being loved rather than controlled are less likely to behave in this way.

Dealing with trying behaviour

Here are the three Ps of dealing with an adolescent who is being a pain:

- Keep it in perspective. Remind yourself that 'This is normal adolescent stuff; there are areas of my and her life that are OK.'
- Don't take it personally. Say to yourself 'This is not targeted at me!'
- It won't persist. Keep the long-term goal in mind: to raise a confident, self-reliant, decent member of society.

Sometmes it's hard to decide which is more infuriating: the pouty resentful expression recognised in most households as 'that face', procrastination, or a seemingly total disregard for lounge-room furniture. Other normal but annoying behaviour that commonly causes conflict in families includes: exuberant outbursts; uncooperativeness and rebellion; obsession with fashion (at its extreme, this includes body piercing and tattoos); wasting time, including inordinately long sessions on the telephone and computer; and playing loud music. Sometimes setting up a tent for your teenager in the backyard and sending her out to live in it forever can be a most tempting idea.

But doing things differently is what becoming a self-confident, self-reliant, mature person is about. It's actually what we want to see happening. Who would want an adolescent always to be amenable and passive? It might be nice and quiet, but it wouldn't be normal. Sometimes our children are merely trying to say, 'Please understand—I'm just trying to express my individuality.'

Parents and young people have differing perspectives on conflict. Parents see mundane conflicts as being about right and wrong, challenges to moral codes, rejection of basic values, and other serious stuff. Adolescents generally think more in terms of personal choices: 'I just wanted to do it. What's the big deal?' How can we sort out these common conflicts constructively? Which conflicts can we resolve by negotiation and which ones do we have to win? Here are some examples:

Turn off that bloody TV, computer, CD player, telephone . . .

Which parents in their right mind would allow a stranger into their home to teach their children three to five hours a day? Yet television does exactly that.
—Dr Victor Strasburger

Picture this: Mum comes home from work very tired and has dinner ready at 7.20 p.m. Her teenagers are watching TV. She says, 'Please switch off the TV.' They don't move. She comes back a minute later and raises her voice. The teenagers grunt, 'This is our favourite TV program. Can't we watch TV during dinner?' Mum says, 'No.' A yelling match develops. The family sits in sullen silence at the dinner table.

The parent requests; the teenager refuses; the parent gets frustrated; the teenager ignores or shouts; the parent responds harshly or gives in—and the teenager learns how to get his own way by using anger or silence destructively. Who can blame him if he then uses similar coercive behaviour at school and with peers?

A better alternative is to sit down at a time when the family is calm to discuss family boundaries and rules, limits to use of the

TV, computer, CD player and telephone, and what time dinner is expected. When the rules are negotiated and the consequences are set out clearly, teenagers get a consistent sense of limits, and common sources of irritation can be avoided. This is better done before the event, rather than during an escalating argument. It is also important, once rules and limits have been set, for parents to apply them consistently.

As one young woman said, 'When everyone knows what they are meant to do with the simple things—bedtimes, waking times, chores, party rules, manners, language and cleanliness—the house runs smoothly. We don't fight over stupid things.' Next time you have a family conflict, try this kind of approach:

- Ask what is really behind the problem.
- List all the solutions everyone can think of, even the silly ones.
- Think of all the advantages and disadvantages of each solution.
- Choose the best solution together.
- Try the solution and then review it later, going through the same process again if it doesn't work.

Jeremy spends too much time glued to the computer. He has little face-to-face contact with other people and is losing sleep, missing school, doing less homework and declining social invitations.

There are various possible solutions to this problem. Computer time is a common source of family conflict. One mother said, 'I have been known to steal the mouse, disconnect things, or just stand in the doorway and stare!' His parents could try that. They could also sell the computer; limit the time Jeremy spends playing on it; reduce his playing of violent games on it; let Jeremy play games only with friends present; play games with Jeremy themselves;

move the computer out of the bedroom; turn the computer off at 9 pm each night.

When the three of them sit down and consider all these suggestions, the advantages and disadvantages become evident:

- Some of Jeremy's homework is done on the computer, so selling it would interfere with school work.
- Playing games with friends and parents would increase Jeremy's social interaction (although Jeremy's parents always lose games and feel defeated!).
- Turning the computer off at the end of the day and moving it out of the bedroom would allow other members of the family to have access to it.
- Both parents work late, so monitoring Jeremy's computer time is unrealistic.

The family decide to turn off the computer at 8 pm every evening and then spend time together as a family. This solution is the easiest to monitor and be consistent about. If the new rule is not complied with, Jeremy agrees that the power cable will be disconnected and confiscated for a week.

When progress is reviewed some weeks later, this approach turns out to have worked!

Computer addiction can lead to:
- Social withdrawal and isolation.
- Sleep deprivation (from staying up late or getting up early to use the computer).
- Poor posture and repetitive strain injury.
- Irregular eating and missing meals.

What about the housework?

Katie, aged thirteen, would pick fights with her younger brothers at the dinner table. A family argument would inevitably develop over sharing housework. One parent would end up ordering Katie to her room.

Asked to explain the real problem, Katie said: 'Mum gets home from work late and we are starving. Dad works a late shift and does not get home until 9 pm. Mum expects me to set the table and do everything around the kitchen. The boys don't have to do any housework. My younger brother, Damian, pulls faces when Mum is not looking. Then I tell him off and it all starts.'

Mum saw the real problem like this: 'Katie makes me feel guilty for working. I work hard all day without a rest and I come home to a house in chaos. Katie only helps if I nag her, and I think I will have to give up work because she is not showing any responsibility.'

Arguments over household chores are common, but there are things you can do to stop them escalating: involve the whole family rather than only the offending adolescent; list *all* the chores in the household and come to an agreement on a fair distribution of responsibility and a system for completing them. Rather than asking for help with chores, which implies a favour, ask for family members to share and to cooperate.

Katie and her parents came up with some possible solutions: they could get a bigger table; they could eat earlier; Mum could give up work; Dad could work an early shift but earn less; Katie could tell Damian nicely not to pull faces; Mum could share the chores evenly between the kids; they could all do the chores together; Katie could offer to do chores before she was asked; they could spend special time together on weekends to make up for the busy week.

After this discussion, Katie said she did not want her mother to give up work or her father to work an earlier shift because she realised it benefited the family—her parents were less stressed when they could pay all the bills and still find some spare cash to go to the movies now and then. This admission greatly relieved Mum's guilt, which led to a calmer handling of future conflicts.

In this process, the family solved the current problem and also learnt a different and more constructive way of solving future conflicts. Katie later explained, 'We used to have arguments and later I didn't know what they were even about. Then my parents started this thing where they'd say, "I feel very hurt when you say that." That makes me stop arguing. I now ask: "You feel really angry about what?" It makes us all stop and think what the real argument is about.'

What if the young person refuses to recognise the problem? What if your child, say, continues to mess up the house, refuses to come home at curfew time, or comes home drunk? Punishments in the form of denying privileges, grounding, fines and extra household chores can be imposed, but it is usually better to do this at a time when everyone is calm and forewarned of the consequences. If anger starts to get out of hand, it is important to bring in a third party, such as an extended-family member, a teacher, a student welfare coordinator or a GP, to give the family a different perspective on things.

Involving children in household chores is an important parenting task—it builds character and helps them learn to be team players. As parenting expert Wendy Mogel sagely says in her book *The Blessing of a Skinned Knee*: 'The lessons we instil by insisting that our children do mundane tasks may very well be the ones that stay with them longest, helping them to become self-reliant adults, responsible community members, and loving parents.'

Will you rescue me?

James recently qualified to play in a top tennis team at school. This was a great achievement, but when he told his parents, a prolonged discussion ensued about the changes they'd have to make in their schedule to drive him to before-school training and weekend tournaments, as well as to his social engagements. James's parents felt taken for granted. They thought James was not showing any responsibility and that he felt entitled to be driven everywhere. But they also worried that he wouldn't be safe taking the bus or train.

The family sat down and talked, and came up with the following options: James could walk to the events; he could give up sport; Mum or Dad could drive him to everything; James could consult the bus timetable; he could ask friends if their parents could share the driving; he could arrange to sleep at a friend's house; he could get a lift to school earlier with a neighbour; he could get his learner's permit as soon as possible so that next year he can drive.

The family listed the main advantages and disadvantages of these potential solutions:

- **Walking would help James get fitter.**
- **Giving up sport would solve the problem, but then he would have another problem—boredom.**
- **His parents couldn't do everything, but they wanted him to be safe.**
- **If he stayed at a friend's house, he would have to be more organised and pack his sports equipment, but it would be good to have a change.**
- **He felt embarrassed to ask his neighbour for a lift, even though she drove past the school on her way to work anyway.**

In the end, the best solution seemed to be a combination of all of the above, except giving up sport. James then listed the steps he'd have to take to achieve the desired outcome: telephone friends and neighbours and speak to the tennis coach; ask the school about buses; ask his parents if they could share some of the driving; get fitter.

Later he reviewed his progress and came up with further ideas, including writing up a roster to remind himself how he was going to get to places and when he needed to be there. James's sporting and social life was now more or less sorted out, but it was hard to fit in his homework, so he now had to think about reprioritising that.

Taking a stand about safety

Leadership takes courage. As parents, we sometimes need to be unpopular. While trusting our children is vital, it does not mean that 'anything goes'. In fact, as we've seen, children feel distinctly insecure without clearly set limits, and eventually interpret a lack of them as a lack of caring. Not having limits is like riding a bicycle over a narrow bridge with no railings. During adolescence kids need limits against which to test themselves and within which they feel secure. They need to know at least what a parent thinks about particular issues. As one teenage girl put it, 'If I don't know what my parents think, how can I do the opposite?'

Rules and responsibilities define a household. They prescribe a family's particular way of living together. In fact, a cohesive family in which the child is expected to play a positive, clearly defined role is said to be the strongest thing a kid has going for it. Parents don't have to insist on every little rule: we can always compromise on less world-shattering issues, such as where the soap is supposed to be put in the bathroom. But on the really important matters, we have to take a stand.

Limits are not idle threats, not harsh and unreasonable demands, nor 'here today and gone tomorrow' suggestions. Effective limits are firm, fair, explicit and consistent, and this is what we should aim for. However, limits do need to change over time. There's no special way to manage this evolution, and approaches to it vary greatly. Most parents find that they need to renegotiate the rules every now and then. As teenagers grow up, there's always something new to contend with. One old perennial is: 'What time will you be home?'

For younger adolescents, home time is an issue of safety and must be enforced. As teenagers develop, independence is a value on which they invariably flex their muscles. But parents are still right to ask, 'What time will you be getting home? Or, 'What time do you think would be reasonable? I want to know where you are.' Parents can explain: 'While we're together we're accountable for each other. Would you like it if I were to go off and you didn't know where I was or when I was coming home?'

Fourteen-year-old Susie and her friend, on holidays in a beach town, disappeared after a family dinner and had not returned home by 11.30 pm. Susie's parents had no idea where she was, and her father, who was increasingly worried and angry, went to the local surf lifesaving club, where he suspected she might be. He was told that Susie and her girlfriend had been there earlier but had gone off with a group of older guys to a house party. The father, becoming increasingly agitated, went to the address he was given and found an unsupervised party in full swing and his daughter and her girlfriend in a darkened back room. He ordered them home immediately, saying, 'How dare you put your mother and me in such a worrying situation.' Susie stormed out, shouting, 'I will never speak to you again.'

Several days later, having been grounded, Susie confided in her dad that she knew she was doing the wrong thing and that he and her mother would not have allowed her to go to that particular party. But she was grateful that her dad had acted 'like I thought you would' because she was beginning to feel out of her depth. She said, 'I knew you would react like that, and you only did it because you cared for me.'

Parents can negotiate pledges of safety with teenagers. Here are two suggested by a Member of Parliament at the New South Wales Alcohol Abuse Summit in 2003:

Parents' pledge for safety

- We agree to pick you up any time, day or night, from anywhere, for any reason, to give you a safe ride home.
- We agree not to be critical of any behaviour that leads to the call; just call and we will come.
- If need be, we will give any of your friends a lift home.
- We agree to discuss any matters arising from our pledge in a calm and rational manner.

Teenagers' counterpledge for safety

- We agree not to drive while affected by alcohol or otherwise intoxicated, or while tired or otherwise impaired.
- We agree to call you if we need assistance, regardless of the time, place, or reason.
- We agree not to accept a lift from anyone we suspect of being intoxicated, tired, or an inadequate driver.

Pledges can be developed around other safety issues, such as wearing a bike helmet, sex, smoking, alcohol and other drugs. The important thing about negotiating a pledge is the discussion that inevitably ensues and the opportunity for parents and kids to talk together about safety concerns.

What if a teenager lies to us about where they've been or what they've been doing? We can say something gentle but powerful, like, 'I would like to know why you felt you couldn't tell me the truth.'

Parties: Be there and be fair

Parties at your home require another set of rules. The best idea is to negotiate beforehand what's acceptable and what's not, agree to maintain a friendly, arm's length presence, and trust your offspring and their friends to be a bit responsible. Mostly, it works out OK. Some of the questions to consider:

- Have you spoken to (warned) the neighbours?
- How have you invited people? And could this invitation be forwarded to many people?
- Is there a finishing time? If so, put this on the invitation.
- Have you registered your party with the police?
- Who is supervising? Do you need to hire security?
- Have you manned all possible entrances of the house or venue?
- How many people are coming?
- Should entry be by invitation only?
- Where are people going to leave their valuables?
- Have you considered fire safety?
- In which parts of your home is the party going to take place?
- How will people make their way home?
- What will you do in the event of drugs, alcohol, smoking?

- Are you aware of your responsibilities in respect to minors consuming alcohol in your home?
- How will you prevent people from gate-crashing?

You can register your party directly with your local police station. This will help to prevent the party from being closed down and will ensure that police are aware of the party should any trouble arise. Alternatively, in Sydney, Point Zero Youth Services can register the party with police for you. Their social workers can discuss any concerns you may have in relation to having a house party and elaborate on the questions above. (See Appendix, p. 206)

There are many questions to address, but your teenager will really appreciate the effort you are going to—even if she thinks you a complete dag. It's important to talk these issues over before the party and try to prevent as many things as possible that could go wrong.

In the days before the internet, a mum and dad were delivering their fourteen-year-old daughter and a friend to a local party. As they approached the party address, they saw hordes of older teenagers with armsful of six-packs of beer. The scene at the house was a milling crowd with no adult in sight. The father knocked on the door and discovered that the parents of the host had locked themselves in. The young host had handed out invitations to his party at the local train station! The arriving parents, shocked and angry, immediately took their daughter and her friend back home and called the police to report a party out of control. Later that night there was a violent incident at the party in which someone drew a knife.

What if a parent just feels really angry?
A father often became very angry with his two teenage sons, and would let them know about it—often in no uncertain terms. Mostly,

they were just being adolescent, giving a bit of cheek, taking their time over chores and so on. But this dad was a screamer, and the fact that his wife generally sided with the kids added to his frustration, sadness and disappointment. He felt that he had tried to do his best by them and considered them grossly unappreciative.

Parents frequently argue about how to discipline and generally manage their adolescent children. In this case, Mum believed that Dad's anger was actually stoking the boys' misbehaviour. While this probably was a factor, it is more likely that the boys were acting out their parents' marital difficulties. If these parents had been able to stop blaming each other long enough to find some middle ground or get professional help, their mutual support might have gone a long way towards easing the intergenerational conflict as well.

Conflict happens in every family. When there is a lot of anger involving parents and teenagers, however, it may be serving as a way of channelling or displacing emotional pain. As teenagers separate from their parents as part of the process of growing up, these feelings inevitably surface, and there is sadness and distress on both sides. So it makes sense that some people will fight together rather than face the feelings of loss associated with moving apart.

Of course, when the fighting becomes constant or is tinged with cruelty, or when it starts to affect the health of a family member or extends beyond the family—to school failure, for example—it is time to take stock. Someone, perhaps Mum and Dad together, needs time out, or the family needs professional help. Remember, too, that irritability and anger are common features of depression.

As our dear friend the late Bronwyn Donaghy once said: 'Persevere—don't give up. Have proper conversations; listen and show respect; know what is normal and when to worry; hug your kids. Just get in there and hold on.'

The messages to remember

We can use family conflict as an opportunity to teach teenagers a better process for working through problems. It goes like this:

- Consider, all together as a family, if possible, what is really behind the problem.

- List all the solutions you can think of, even the silly ones.

- List all the advantages and disadvantages of each solution.

- Choose the best solution.

- Try the solution and then review it later.

- Go through the same process again if it doesn't work.

- Most of all, parents should teach by example, set limits, take a stand on issues of safety, and always keep communication lines open.

6
Parents and adolescents— dealing with stress

Concern should drive us into action not depression.

—Karen Honey

Adolescence can be stressful. With pressures coming from all directions, inside and out, growing up can feel like navigating your way through a maze. Unfortunately, many of the signposts that could make this process easier are hidden from view. Teenagers do not always get the help and guidance they need.

Parents, simply by being parents, sometimes add to the stresses their children face. But even if it were possible to magically create a stress-free environment at home, it would be undesirable. Stress is an unavoidable part of life, and children need to learn how to deal with it. But we can do much to lessen the blows, particularly during the early teen years, when young people are still developing inner strength and resilience. One important way is to listen to their problems and understand their point of view. Make home a sanctuary, a safe place where they can be themselves. Like Jack, aged fourteen said:

I felt really empty and I told my mum. I said, 'I don't even know how I feel, but I feel nothing today.' She just sat me down and replied, 'Don't worry, it's normal to feel that way sometimes. Be kind to yourself. Have a little rest and a drink of water and come and talk to me'. It was just a small thing but now, when I feel that way, I just repeat my mum's words inside my head and things feel normal again.

Pressure in itself is not the problem. If it motivates us and we can control it, it is clearly a positive force. Particularly when there is an end in sight, pressure can lead to the pride of accomplishment and a boost in morale. This type of stress is desirable and healthy.

But when pressure is prolonged and we cannot manage it, things are very different. We may feel as if we are choking or drowning in worries, and start showing signs of being 'stressed out'. We may feel anxious or tense, as if we're revved up with nowhere to go. We may get a dry mouth, pounding heart, butterflies in the stomach and a sense of impending doom. Our muscles tense up, resulting in discomforts such as headache, backache and abdominal pain.

Prolonged stress is damaging to the body, either directly or indirectly, in the following ways:

- **Blood pressure is increased and fats are released into the bloodstream**
- **The immune system is suppressed**
- **There is a greater likelihood of physical illness**
- **Highly stressed people are also more likely to have accidents**

Why is adolescence stressful?

If we all experience stress, why should we be particularly concerned about adolescents? In the past, theorists such as Anna Freud

(Sigmund's daughter) described adolescence as a time of 'storm and stress'. In their view, it was actually abnormal for adolescents to be normal; the turmoil of this phase of life was essential for growth and development. This view is outdated. Research shows that not all young people are in storm and stress; in general, about 20 per cent of teenagers (far too many) report themselves to be persistently unhappy, troubled or in turmoil. Nevertheless, for all sorts of reasons, adolescence is a challenging time.

A confusing and competitive world

These days, we're all affected by what is happening around the world. And it's a world filled with change and uncertainty. The media bring us a constant flow of bad news, of strife and destruction and inhumanity. Our windows on the world of television and the internet often do anything but create a sense of peace and security.

As young people come alive to what is going on in the wider world, no wonder they are touched with dismay. Having less to look back upon than adults, they are greatly concerned with the future. And things are moving and changing so fast. How can teenagers figure out where they fit into the scheme of things if nothing around them keeps still?

Young people also find themselves in a society focused on individualism, productivity and competitiveness. Child and adolescent psychiatrist Professor Ken Nunn encourages a sense of perspective:

> Every kid needs to know they have a niche. In the big swim of life, most of us are happy with a puddle. Not all of us want to be a salmon going up the waterfall, knowing there's a bear waiting to catch you on the way up. And when you get up there, you reproduce and then you die. In the dominant model

of competitiveness in our society, either you're a salmon or a little, meaningless squiggle at the bottom.

He's right. Not all of us want to be salmon. Not all of us want to be a big fish or make that high climb. Yet who wants to feel like a meaningless squiggle? It's a tough world, but it's one in which teenagers must find a place somehow. Of course, there's not a lot that parents can do about the larger, global currents that sweep us along. But caring adults at home and at school who provide a sense of connectedness and belonging—and a community that does the same—can help teenagers face and adapt to everyday causes of stress.

Living up to expectations

Teenagers say they feel a lot of pressure to live up to the expectations of their families, friends, school and society, and their own expectations as well. Some of these are real, some only perceived. Teenagers are influenced by information or misinformation from their peers, the media and parents. These pressures are often inadvertent, unintended or unspoken. They may cause unnecessary stress and tend to be different for males and females.

One class of Year 10 boys wrote this list of conflicting expectations:

- to be role models to siblings
- to be interested in cars and sport
- to succeed at school and have career aspirations
- to be tough and brave
- to have big muscles and abs
- to have body odour
- to be interested in the opposite sex
- to get a car, house, wife, kids, job, etc.
- to rebel and live on the wild side.

A class of Year 10 girls compiled this list:

- to be feminine and pretty, skinny, to have boobs and good teeth but no pimples, cellulite or body hair
- to like guys, not girls, and not be a lesbian
- to be smart, but not too smart
- to finish school, get a good job and have kids
- to be rich
- to have sex when a guy wants you to and to provide protection such as condoms or the Pill
- to not have sex
- to smoke if everyone else does so they will be friends with you
- to be perfect
- never to burp or fart.

It's clear that some of these pressures of expectation come from teenagers' own minds rather than from parents or teachers, but that doesn't make them any less stressful. When we talk to teenagers, we can be aware of these expectations, ask them to make their own list and perhaps talk about which ones are real and which are not.

A time of inner conflict

Set against other people's expectations of us are our inner drives. Teenagers don't necessarily want to meet all the expectations they feel under pressure to conform to. They have natural talents and interests that may push them in different directions. Sometimes, however, following inner drives can bring even more stress. This is especially true of those who are developing an attraction to members of the same sex. Young gay men are often teased and sense hostility and rejection from their peers, family and community. This can put them at risk of depression and even suicide.

Reconciling inner drives with outer expectations is a balancing act requiring great skill and finesse. It's not easy to find a path between personal opinions, natural inclinations, peer pressure and parental expectations. The conflicts teenagers have to resolve include:

- **The need to express themselves as individuals versus peer pressure to conform**
- **The need to compete with their friends versus the need to win social approval**
- **The need to achieve independence versus the need for parental support and validation**

It's little surprise, then, that teenagers behave erratically at times. After all, it's impossible to please all the people (themselves included) all the time! Unbeknown to others—or even themselves, sometimes—teenagers are constantly practising the subtle art of compromise perhaps without even being aware of it themselves. What will be noticeable to them, though, is the stress involved. Remember, too, that adolescence is a time of new experiences and new feelings, of strong attachments and bitter losses. It is a time of demands and frustrations. Under normal circumstances, teenagers are stressed by practically everything, from their rapidly changing bodies and wondering what is or isn't normal, to the feeling that nobody understands or listens; from the pressure of exams or other performances to the usual hassles with Mum and Dad.

Here's what teenagers say about stress and how they cope with it.

It's important to find a balance with friends, study and personal space. I think to myself, 'This is only a small hurdle in life—I will feel good about myself once I have done it and I will have achieved something.' My family will accept me and will be proud of me even if I don't do well. I worry that everyone else will be judging the outcome.

I think before I begin something stressful—I can only try my best. I only get stressed out if I compare myself to others. Small things can tip the stress scales—like not having enough hours in the day, the pressure to conform to rules and expectations. I have learnt not to jump to conclusions when things go wrong.

When I am doing something stressful, I think: 'It will be over soon and if something goes wrong, it's not the end of the world and my mother won't really kill me.' And no matter what, if I've tried my best I can never do better than that. It feels worse if I think: 'What if I mess this up?' I try to make myself feel better by thinking positively. There are two quotes I love: 'Only dead fish go with the flow,' and 'Have the courage to live, anyone can die'.

In a stressful situation, I try to focus on the moment but remind myself that what I am doing is going to help me in the future and I will be proud of myself afterwards. There is always the fear that things won't turn out the way I hope, but because I have learnt to pace myself, I am confident I have at least tried my hardest. I think as long as you work hard to gain something, you can expect it to work out. It's when we sit back and wait for things to come to us and do not try that we lose out. It's about taking a step forwards and facing the fear of the unknown. Not knowing what will happen once you take that step is scary, but each step gets us closer to where we really want to be. If you set your own goals, you will achieve them. No one will talk you out of them.

Thinking depressed

Parents teach their children ways of thinking and communicating. When parents are asked to speak for several minutes about their child, the number of negative things they say can be a rough guide to the amount of negativity the child is being exposed to on a daily basis. Teenagers can pick up this negativity and begin to think about themselves and their lives in predominantly negative terms. They may see things in black-and-white, either-or terms rather than as a continuum with a lot of middle and grey areas.

One teenager described it like this: 'I have all these negative thoughts. That I have no real future. That I will fail miserably in my future job. That I am a terrible person. The thought of gaining weight. Embarrassment. The thought of someone demanding respect from me when they don't respect me to begin with. The thought of losing the people I love and confronting the people I dislike. I don't know how I got all these fears, but they are constantly in my mind.'

Negative rumination (repeatedly going over the same negative thoughts) is a big part of what we call thinking depressed. Often, the thoughts are self-lacerating and critical. When self-judgement dominates thinking, it creates a harsh inner monologue—an inner scold. Fear and doubt lead to a shaky sense of self. Thinking depressed erodes young people's resilience and has real and damaging effects in everyday life. For example, if a child thinks she looks ugly she may spend less time with friends. Spending less time with friends makes her feel lonely and so on, down a spiral of depression (see Chapter 11).

In many cases, we are blissfully unaware of the negative thoughts in the minds of our sons or daughters or of their everyday consequences. We as parents can help by examining our own negative thinking and guiding teenagers to do the same. Here are some questions to consider:

- Am I only noticing the negative side of things?
- Am I worrying about things I can't do anything about?
- Am I taking things personally?
- Do I exaggerate things?
- What lies behind my thinking?
- Am I blaming myself for things that are not my fault?
- Am I seeking solutions or just complaining?
- Is this thinking helpful or unhelpful?
- Am I assuming things can't change?
- Does my thinking lead to good or bad consequences?

On the other hand, parents who think positively transmit a positive, upbeat attitude. Here are some suggestions for prompting positive thoughts:

- Make a note of things that went well today.
- Write down the things about you that are strong.
- Doing good is good for you—write a thank you letter or do something unexpectedly kind for someone every week.
- How is your life? What are your life dreams?
- Imagine your best possible self ten years from now and describe who you see.

Helping teenagers deal with stress

Adults have become very interested in stress management. Clearly, though, the earlier stress-minimising habits and skills are learned the better. It is generally accepted that:

- People with strong support systems and a strong sense of connectedness and caring live longer and suffer less stress-related disease than those who feel isolated and lonely.

- Certain lifestyle habits are helpful in strengthening us against the effects of stress: a sensible diet, adequate sleep and regular exercise; an ability to slow down and do one thing at a time; and a reasonable balance between work, rest and play.

Throughout childhood, parents can encourage kids to view pressure as a challenge, to cope with hard knocks courageously and well, and to develop skills for dealing with the more serious threats to their emotional equilibrium. Much has been written on this subject, but there are four main keys:

Rehearsal. It is extremely important for children and teenagers to be able to anticipate stressful or challenging situations they might encounter and mentally practise possible solutions. It is good to have fantasies and daydreams, to practise things in your mind and to imagine oneself in various situations: happy, tense, stressful and fearsome. Watching movies, acting in plays or reading novels can also be effective ways of learning how to cope with the challenges of life.

Relaxation. Being able to relax is a potent antidote to stress and a major advantage to a young person facing, say, an exam or a public performance (such as giving a speech or going for a job interview). Since Transcendental Meditation was introduced to the West in the early 1960s, millions of people throughout the world have taken up various styles of meditation in order to achieve a state of conscious restfulness. Teenagers might not be too taken with this approach, but knowing at least how to physically relax quickly is useful for almost anyone.

A quick relaxation technique: Take several slow, deep breaths, relaxing the shoulders while breathing out. Gradually allow your breathing to become quieter and more peaceful. Relax the muscles of your face and jaw. Once your facial expression becomes tranquil and at ease, the mind and body tend to follow.

Positive self-talk. When things go wrong, most people put themselves down ('I probably deserved it, anyway'). Positive self-talk is the opposite, a marvellous mental tool for building self-control and confidence in the face of adversity ('Well, I tried my best in the ballet exam—next time will be better').

Assertiveness. This is probably the most important anti-stress attribute we can have, but it's one whose value we tend to underestimate. Assertiveness simply means saying and doing what is right for you without being aggressive or threatening in situations where there is pressure to do otherwise. Assertiveness is about communicating effectively in situations of stress. If that means saying 'No' (the most important assertiveness tool of all), then that's what you say. A young person who is assertive also tends to be confident he can solve problems. In the jargon of psychology, he has self-efficacy. Such teenagers will say, for example, that they're pretty sure they can handle a specific problem, such as not sleeping well. That inner confidence makes them much less likely to get depressed and more likely to recover from a bout of depression.

The messages to remember

- Positive thinking prevents depression

- Learning to relax protects against stress

- Challenging negative thoughts improves self-worth and self-control

- Being assertive builds self-confidence and guards against depression

7

Helping adolescents stay healthy

If they had their way, they'd probably try to live on soft drink, chips and chocolate. And to our chagrin they would probably survive.
—David Bennett and Leanne Rowe

True as that oft-made observation is, a healthy lifestyle—and a diet that isn't all soft drink, chips and chocolate—is, as we know, important for teenagers. It helps give them the bounce of resilience and protect them from depression. The good news is that caring adults can help adolescents stay healthy. Simple things can work wonders here: keeping healthy foods in the fridge and having fruit bowls around the home, encouraging young people to make their own fresh school lunch and to choose water and low-fat milk over other drinks. Modelling healthy behaviour is also key. Young people are much more likely to exercise regularly if their parents and teachers do too. Family weekend activities based around exercise and sport also help promote healthy young minds and bodies.

Knowing about good nutrition

Nutrition is constantly being written about in magazines and books, the health food industry is booming, and the importance of weight control and healthy eating is on almost everybody's mind. Most people know something about anorexia nervosa and that there are good reasons for concern about chronic constipation, obesity and high blood cholesterol levels.

Most children under eleven eat breakfast, but by adolescence about 40 per cent of girls and 30 per cent of boys skip breakfast regularly. Many teenagers say it's a matter of simply not feeling hungry in the morning or running out of time. Girls in particular may be avoiding breakfast in the misguided belief that it will help them control their weight. It doesn't—mostly because they get hungry and eat more at other meals. Furthermore, studies show that it is harder to concentrate on school work with nothing in your stomach—an argument that may or may not have the desired effect! More importantly, kids who miss breakfast are more likely than their breakfast-eating peers to be lacking calcium and iron, at an age when they need both most. This is where the good old banana smoothie can come to the rescue, or a grab-it-and-go nutritious snack.

As we all know, fast food is a way of life for young people. They rarely have time to do more than quickly chew the food they gobble on the run. Gentle digestion—forget it. This wouldn't matter if most takeaway foods were not so energy-rich and packed with fat and salt. Salt makes fast food more palatable encouraging one to eat more, as well as making people crave a drink—all too often a soft drink. Of course, if adults demanded a higher standard things might change, but for now, we're stuck with what the fast-food industry chooses to call 'meeting consumer demand'.

Then there's the matter of what teenagers wash all the junk food down with. Gone are the days when a drink meant milk or water. Now it's more likely to be soft drinks or beer. Caffeine-based drinks can be addictive, and highly acidic colas can damage tooth enamel if consumed to excess. It's astounding that there is not more public debate about addiction to such drinks, which are marketed seductively. They are the ultimate synthetic food, 'that wonderful junction where science meets food: kilojoule-free, nutrient-free, and vaguely immoral'.

School canteens ought to limit the availability of soft drinks and junk food. It makes no sense for good nutrition to be taught in the classroom if high-fat and poor food choices are available in the canteen. Some healthy choices should be on offer, such as fruit, fruit salad, low-fat flavoured milk, yoghurt and nutritious sandwiches. Similar concerns relate to vending machines and the sorts of food available at sporting and recreational venues.

What are the basics of good nutrition?

Healthy meals are based on high-fibre carbohydrate foods such as whole-grain breads and cereals (oats, barley, psyllium, porridge, untoasted muesli), legumes (dried beans, lentils or chickpeas), raw vegetables, salads (leafy green vegetables, carrots, tomatoes, and cruciferous vegetables like broccoli, cabbage, brussels sprouts, bok choy and other Asian greens) and fruit (citrus fruits are particularly high in antioxidants).

Foods containing calcium (skim milk and tofu) and iron (lean meat, dark green vegetables) are encouraged, while saturated fat (fatty meat, full cream dairy products), sugar and salt are discouraged. Healthy snacks include fruit, wholegrain bread, fruit bread, high-fibre biscuits, low-fat milk or yoghurt. Two or more serves of oily fish per week are recommended. Fat, salt and sugar can be cut down, simply by not having junk foods and soft drinks at home.

It is important to have at least three meals a day, including a nutritious breakfast. Cereals like Weetbix or untoasted muesli, wholegrain toast, eggs and fruit provide a good start to the day. Vegetarians need to eat foods rich in protein and iron such as nuts, chickpeas, lentils and baked beans.

Good nutrition doesn't just keep us bright eyed and bushy tailed. It prevents obesity and serious illnesses, such as cardiovascular disease and Type 2 diabetes. Equally important for teenagers is the effect of nutrition on mood and behaviour. The immediate effects of large amounts of sugar and caffeine are obvious. Some artificial colours, particularly tartrazine (yellow colouring, which is also in many red, green and blue drinks and coloured sweets and snacks), can cause agitated and hyperactive behaviour. The longer-term link between poor nutrition and depression is less clear, but important to consider.

Countries where people eat a lot of fish oil tend to have lower incidences of depression than those where little fish oil is eaten. This is supported by a number of studies that have found positive effects on mental function from omega-3 fatty acids. In some studies, sugar avoidance has been found to relieve depression, while others have shown that it has a short-term benefit in lifting mood.

Heavy alcohol drinkers are more likely to develop depression. After a binge people tend to feel low; unfortunately these feelings may be temporarily relieved by drinking more alcohol, thus creating a vicious cycle. Caffeine has been found to increase mood swings and panic attacks in people with anxiety. As your brain is 85 per cent water by weight, it makes sense to keep it adequately hydrated by drinking water rather than colas and energy drinks, which make you pass more urine.

Eating fresh foods like nuts, seeds, fruits, dark leafy vegetables and whole-grain bread support brain function. Soy beans and products like tofu and tempeh are a great source of tryptophan, which helps the brain produce happy hormones associated with emotional well-being and sound sleep.

Young people are susceptible to a range of diet-related health problems, most well known, some potentially dangerous, and practically all preventable. Parents certainly worry, and for good reason, particularly when their children are too thin or when an eating problem becomes an eating disorder. According to Australian studies, one in every 200 girls aged between fifteen and nineteen has anorexia nervosa, and about one in twenty young women has the binge-eating disorder bulimia nervosa. Both occur in boys as well, but more seldom. Being overweight is also a serious threat to health and emotional well-being.

On promoting exercise and fitness

The evidence that regular physical exercise is good for our bodies and minds is pretty impressive. Fitness would seem to have everything going for it:

- With effective muscle control comes better posture.
- With increased physical endurance comes less fatigue.
- Physical activity decreases tension and is therefore an effective way of coping with stress and anxiety.
- Exercise contributes to the enjoyment of leisure time.
- Regular physical exercise helps with weight control and can ward off diabetes, heart attacks and strokes in later life.

The Australian guidelines on physical activity recommend that adolescents get an hour of proper physical activity (you know, the sort that makes you really sweat) every day. It won't surprise many parents or teachers to read that studies of Australian primary and secondary school children rate their general fitness as less than optimal.

While many teenagers do get stuck into sport and exercise, too many others are doing their darnedest to get out of it. For a variety of reasons, a loss of interest in exercise at puberty is not unusual, especially in girls. Possible reasons include other interests, being overweight, a lack of motivation, spending too much time in front of the TV or computer, not doing well in games at school, or a reaction against adults' overemphasis on competitive sports.

Young people who are interested in sport tend to have a healthier body image and are less likely to begin smoking or become pregnant as teenagers. They take greater pride in their physical and social selves than their sedentary peers. They remain more physically active as they age and suffer less depression.

Of course, some people aren't good at sports or just aren't interested. If this describes your teenager, chances are it describes you too—athleticism or lack thereof is often inherited. If your teenager has difficulty hitting a ball with a bat, or is talented at tripping over his feet, certain sports are simply not for him. Young people with such disabilities may not be able to do some activities, while those who are obese need appropriate alternatives. But no one needs to miss out on exercise.

Perhaps the clue to success here is tapping into a child's interests and trying to find some physical activity that they can connect with. A non-althetic type might respond better to yoga or creative dance; an overweight young person might like to join a dog-exercising or training group; a shy child might get involved with a bushcraft group. Who knows what sorts of ideas might start flowing during an enthusiastic open discussion about the options?

This is also a situation when doing things with your child may serve a better purpose than sending her away, as in 'Let's go for a walk together' rather than, 'Off you go and get fit'. This approach kills two birds with one stone: you both get some exercise and also spend time together. You never know, it might even lead to talking and improving your own health too!

The aim in all cases should be to encourage physical activity that can also serve as a source of pleasure. Simple pleasures in a context of sociability such as bushwalking, kite flying or even just mowing the lawn also do you good. Creating such opportunities just means thinking outside the square.

Fatigue and sleep

Young people commonly complain of tiredness. When teenagers are going through their growth spurt, for example, they seem to need more sleep. We're not sure if this is to enable their growing to occur under the influence of nighttime bursts of hormones or because they're using more energy or just because their lifestyle is more tiring.

Whatever the cause, young people need to be taught how to nurture themselves and to refresh their bodies. Often a good meal and a good night's sleep will be all that's required to bring energy levels back to normal. If fatigue persists (say for more than a week), however, a medical check-up is advisable.

Everybody gets physically fatigued at times, usually as a result of overexertion, overwork, lack of sleep, or all of the above. This type of fatigue is transient, improves with rest and is not debilitating.

Many young people do not understand how to settle themselves for sleep. Parents may find these suggestions helpful:

- Avoid alcohol or caffeine-containing drinks (including coffee, chocolate and many soft drinks) near bedtime.
- Do not exercise near bedtime, as this usually raises the heart rate and interferes with sleep. On the other hand, exercise during the day helps release tension and promotes general relaxation and thus sounder sleep.
- In the hour before settling down for sleep, dim the lights, listen to music, read a comforting book, drink a glass of milk (better if warm) or practise some relaxation exercises.

- Finish with TV and homework or anything else that stimulates the mind (including arguments and emotional discussions) at least one hour before bedtime. Sleeping tablets are to be strongly discouraged.

Persistent lack of sleep can cause moodiness, irritability, fatigue and difficulty concentrating (which teachers notice in class), and commonly precedes depression. It is also important to avoid daytime or evening naps, time in bed without sleeping, prolonged inactivity, and rehearsing or worrying about stressful events.

If your teenager is not sleeping well try to help them with this advice. To break the sleep-wake-toss-and-turn cycle, it helps to go to bed only when sleepy. If you lie awake for more than 30 minutes, it's best to get up and do something soothing, even if this needs to be repeated throughout the night. Try to set a routine of getting up at the same time every morning, no matter what time you went to bed or how tired you are. Rather than worrying about sleep, try to accept that you cannot sleep—otherwise it becomes a vicious cycle. Doing some relaxation exercises and more physical exercise throughout the day is preferable.

Smoking—still a problem

Smoking is less common among young people than at any time since the 1980s. Maybe the shock, horror TV ads and cigarette-pack labels are working! But 7 per cent of Australians aged twelve to fifteen and 18 per cent of seventeen-year-olds smoke, so we shouldn't be complacent. Anti-smoking messages have done some good, but it risks being undone by web venues like YouTube, Facebook and MySpace, which are being used to promote smoking in teenagers. Professor Simon Chapman, a public health expert at the University of Sydney, says: 'There is a huge amount of pro-tobacco material on the web which escapes regulation. This is the new battleground for the lungs of our adolescents.'

Youth smoking remains a major concern because it is so addictive and has such serious effects on long-term health. For girls it takes on average three weeks of smoking to become addicted; for boys, about six months. Some adolescents have a genetic vulnerability that means they become addicted unusually quickly. In their case, just experimenting with tobacco may lead rapidly to nicotine dependence. And of course, the earlier smoking commences (nine out of ten smokers start while they are still children) the harder it is to give up, and the more likely it is that early complications will develop.

Girls tend to use smoking as a way—however ineffective—to cope with stress. A possible reason for this is that they may feel adolescent tensions and conflicts somewhat more sharply than boys. Some girls also believe smoking will keep them thin. Girls appear on the whole to be more influenced than boys by positive images of smoking in magazines. We also know that parental attitudes and behaviour make a big difference—the risk that a child will smoke rises threefold if his parents smoke, but decreases if parents disapprove of smoking or quit themselves.

Important Australian research links cigarette smoking with other substance use (especially alcohol and marijuana) and poor mental health. Girls who smoke, in particular, are much more likely to be anxious and depressed than those who don't.

Alcohol—a clear and present danger

Drinking among adolescents is a serious problem. Alcohol is a depressant, but its initial effect is to relax you and remove inhibitions. This temporary loosening-up may make it easier to feel part of the peer group. Young people today start younger, drink more and indulge in binge drinking to a greater extent than previous generations. Around 70 per cent of sixteen- to seventeen-year-olds report that they drink alcohol, and alcohol dependence and its complications are increasingly common. The law prohibits under-age drinking. Alcohol may not be sold to people under eighteen, even at private parties as part of a food package. Even though minors found drinking on licensed premises may be prosecuted, this does not seem to decrease the problem.

Boys and girls have very similar rates of alcohol consumption, even in their mid-teens. The girls have caught up over the years, proof that the stigma once attached to female drinking has all but disappeared in Australia. The young teenagers of twenty years ago who furtively drank beer and a limited range of spirits would not recognise the abundance of new brands now on liquor store shelves. These include ready-made cocktails and fruit-based alcoholic drinks that appeal to the under-thirties (let's hear it for advertising), particularly young women who dislike the taste of booze. Many drinks now have dedicated websites featuring computer games, competitions, jokes and marketing strategies that include the distribution of free beer samples at over-eighteen-year-olds' parties.

What do teenagers say about alcohol?

Some people act like they are drunk to get attention but this is really sad. Girls use alcohol to be more relaxed and confident. When you go to a new school, you want new friends and so you do things to fit in.

It's become the thing to do on a weekend to drink alcohol. Some people become really aggressive when they are drunk and they use it as an excuse for bad behaviour. Some people drink just to spite their parents, especially when they've been told not to.

The main reasons young people drink are to fit in or to relax. For many, partying with alcohol and marijuana is part of an adolescent rite of passage. Wherever did they get the idea that you have to drink to relax? Notwithstanding our concerns about alcohol advertising, research shows that, as with smoking, Australian teenagers who drink are much more likely to report that both parents drink, and are more likely to have been offered their first drink by parents or relatives. Surveys have found that when young people are asked what influences their decision to drink or not drink, more than 60 per cent say their parents are the main influence with 28 per cent saying it's their peers.

What's depressing about all this is that drinking to excess can seriously damage health. And even mild to moderate drinking adversely affects the development of a young brain and body. About 3700 Australians die and more than 70 000 are admitted to hospital each year because of complications related to alcohol abuse. It has recently been estimated that the net social costs of alcohol abuse in Australia total over $7.5 billion a year in terms of health costs, effects on employment and productivity, family breakdown and crime.

The National Health and Medical Research Council recommends that people under eighteen avoid alcohol. For those over eighteen, it recommends no more than two standard drinks per day and at least two alcohol-free days a week. However, new research shows that even this level of drinking may adversely affect the growing brain up to the age of 25 years. A drinking problem is measured not only by how much a person drinks, but also by how the drinking affects his or her life and the lives of people around them.

The acute problems are bad enough: drunkenness, accidents, violence, arrests and unprotected sex (girls in particular are more likely to be victims of sexual abuse). Binge drinkers can die from alcohol poisoning—blood levels in excess of 0.3 milligrams per

100 ml (six times the legal driving limit) can be fatal—or from choking on their own vomit. Everybody, adults and teenagers alike, should know how to get someone who's unconscious or 'out of it' into the recovery position. Teenage deaths from toxic overdose have usually involved a dare to down a bottle of spirits. For most young drinkers, however, it's dangerous behaviour and drink driving that pose the greatest threat to life—teenagers are learning to drink at around the same time as they're learning to drive.

Longer term problems are less obvious, although regular drinking in adolescence is now recognised as an important risk factor for developing abusive, dependent and risky patterns of drinking behaviour later. Also, people who drink regularly may become dependent on alcohol or develop a tolerance to it, so they need more to get the same effect. The health consequences of chronic alcohol abuse include cirrhosis of the liver, some cancers, chronic malnutrition and the risk of infection and, of course, brain damage. Yes, heavy drinking shrinks your brain in the long term—it causes an irreversible loss of cortical tissue and dementia.

Parents won't have too much trouble noticing when a teenager staggers home reeking of alcohol or wakes up with a hangover. But there are some other early warning signs that drinking may be getting out of hand: increased moodiness and aggressiveness, shaky hands, sleeplessness and anxiety, and deteriorating school or work performance, none of which, of course, are exclusive to alcohol abusers.

Parents who are worried about their teenager's drinking can get advice from their local Community Health Centre, many of which employ specialist drug and alcohol workers, or call a twenty-four-hour drug and alcohol information service. For a very sick or unconscious teenager who's been drinking, the best thing to do—after getting them on their side with chin tilted and slightly raised—is to call a doctor or an ambulance.

Other drugs

Young people take drugs for much the same variety of reasons that adults do: to get high usually in a social setting, to be part of the group, to relieve boredom or gain relief from emotional pain, anxiety, depression and family problems, to escape the boundaries of ordinary experience, or simply to relax, reduce the pressure and slow down. Young people generally start off by experimenting with a drug, often to find out what it feels like, as part of general risk-taking or rebellion, but it may become a habit when they think it solves—or helps them forget about—their problems.

- Teenagers generally know a lot more about drug use today than in times past. It is glorified in popular culture, the use of needles has lost some of its junkie associations, and young people are less afraid of experimenting with drugs.
- Young people today are often multiple drug users.
- Teenagers abuse easy-to-access over-the-counter drugs such as cough medicine containing codeine, analgesics like paracetamol, antihistamines and decongestants, all of which may be dangerous if taken incorrectly.
- Young people sometimes steal drugs from the family medicine cabinet and sell them as party drugs. Common household products are being inhaled by some teenagers and can be deadly.
- Many high school students take tranquillisers such as Serepax and Valium for stress-related symptoms. These drugs are frequently abused by kids whose parents use them.
- Prescription drugs such as Dexamphetamine and Ritalin, used in the treatment of ADHD, are more

available in schools these days, and are being abused as stimulants by teenagers who don't have the disorder.

- Cannabis and LSD now exist in more potent forms than were available in the past, and have serious side effects such as mental illness.
- Dance parties are characterised by the use of hallucinogenic drugs such as ecstasy and clubbing by the use of stimulant drugs such as crystal meth, which can cause severe psychological problems and occasionally death.
- Home laboratories for manufacturing methamphetamine (speed) have made this drug much more widely available.

Despite the known dangers of the most common drugs, alcohol and tobacco, it's illegal drugs that worry parents the most. Of these, cannabis (marijuana) is the most popular overall and the most used by young people. There is good evidence that cannabis can cause depression and that it interferes with the treatment of depression.

What are the signs of drug use? There is no precise profile of a drug-taking adolescent, or any other type of drug taker, in fact. A lot depends on what they're taking, how much, and in what circumstances. Mood swings and changes in behaviour patterns may be symptoms of drug abuse but, as we've seen, these may also be entirely normal. What we do know is that young people who misuse drugs go to great lengths to conceal their use. The smarter and more alert their parents, the harder they try to cover it up. For more information on illicit drugs refer to Chapter 16.

Benefits of family meals

Research conducted in Minneapolis, Minnesota USA has shown that eating meals together as a family benefits teenagers above and beyond the general sense of connectedness that family mealtimes engender. Frequent family meals correlated with better academic achievement and less depression, as well as with less tobacco, alcohol and marijuana use. The findings suggest that eating family meals may enhance the health and wellbeing of adolescents and should be recommended.

The messages to remember

- Good nutrition and regular exercise are essential for a healthy mind and body.

- Parents are the role models that teenagers watch most closely. The way you eat and exercise, and your attitudes to drinking, smoking and other drug use can have a powerful influence. It's up to you to make that influence a good one.

- Good sleep patterns are important for the growing teenager. Young people need to be taught how to nurture themselves and refresh their bodies.

8
Making school a positive, not a problem

I am enough of an artist to draw freely upon my imagination. Imagination is more important than knowledge. Knowledge is limited. Imagination encircles the world.

—Albert Einstein

What makes a good school?

A good school for teenagers is one that fulfils their most important and basic needs: receiving a good education and training in life skills; having good friends; having good teachers; believing that they fit in at school; feeling respected by their teachers; having a safe adult other than a parent take an interest in them. As one girl put it, 'Everyone at school backs me up: my friends, their parents, the teachers, even the canteen ladies.'

A good school connects with families and the community and looks after its teachers. It teaches the three Rs but encourages a love of learning, creativity (art, theatre, music, creative writing and poetry), leadership, citizenship, participation and contribution, sport, community service, social responsibility, ethics and debating. Quality in a school is not about what it looks like, but what it feels like. A good school feels positive and safe.

There is also the matter of a 'good fit' between the school or class and the student, which often depends on the focus and atmosphere of the school. Sometimes it helps to change schools when problems arise, but it is generally better in the long run to teach teenagers to persevere and overcome whatever problems they may be having. As Richard Eckersley says in *Well & Good*: 'The fundamental task of education today is not just to prepare students for the future, but to equip them to create the future they want to live in . . . More should and could be done in schools to encourage in young people a greater sense of optimism about the future, a conviction that the future is theirs to shape, and the faith in themselves needed to tackle the task'.

What makes a good teacher?

Teachers are doing more good than they possibly realise when they do simple things like remembering a student's name, giving a smile or a wink when passing in the corridor, or showing a little extra interest. Warmth, concern and care from a teacher can be more effective than even a session with the school counsellor in terms of giving to a young person an indication that they are acknowledged, understood and nurtured. Albert Einstein clearly had at least one good teacher. He once said: 'It is the supreme art of the teacher to awaken joy in creative expression and knowledge.' Apparently that wasn't the case for Woody Allen, who remarked, 'I had a terrible education. I attended a school for emotionally disturbed teachers.'

What is a good teacher? There is no single, universally accepted answer. Is it someone who knows his subject and can bring that knowledge alive for students? Is it someone who cracks jokes from time to time and shows a human face? Probably these things and more. Adolescents need room to move as individuals, and greatly value a teacher who provides it. They also need positive reinforcement and someone they can trust. One English teacher encourages her students to communicate with her, if they like, through a journal. They can write to her about anything at all, knowing they will get back a caring comment, a few simple words of encouragement or advice. They would probably describe her as a good teacher.

Some parents are intimidated by teachers and avoid them at all costs. Parent–teacher nights come and go and they stay at home. For those who do attend, however, meeting our child's teacher can be extremely informative and worthwhile. Teachers feel the same way. Knowing who a student's parents are, they say, makes a difference to their attitude to the student, who then becomes more than just a face in the crowd. The triangular relationship between school, child and parent is an extremely important one and educators are certain that their efforts are more potent when parents are aware, encouraging and involved in what's happening. When we take this step we can get things into better perspective and our teenagers, who'll be aware that we've taken the trouble, cannot help but feel good. Here are some positive comments by young people about teachers:

I need to be given guidance from teachers, with efficient studying and extra privileges when I do well. The teachers are genuinely interested in my work and wellbeing and give me constant help and advice. I was also invited into the staff room for cups of tea. But they made me realise it is up to me to pass Year 12.

The best thing about the final years of school is the improved relationship between teachers and students. My teachers show they respect me by speaking to me and treating me as an adult or friend. I feel like a person, not just a student, when teachers outwardly praise a well-earned achievement, remember my name or make the effort to make conversation. Teachers can be snappy and sometimes so can students. They need to understand that we all have bad days. Teachers should explain things in detail rather than criticise me.

I put a lot of pressure on myself. When I'm doing something difficult, I always think of the hardest thing I've ever done. Then I think, well, if I can do that, I can do this too.

As school goes on I have more independence, more responsibility and more fun. Teachers should make themselves more approachable and be more patient, no matter how stupid my problems are. Giving me the benefit of the doubt is really important. There should be an acknowledgement of my own ability to use common sense and do the right thing.

Here are some negative comments:

Students need to be dealt with individually. Teachers shouldn't try to make superficial conversation to try to show off that they know how to get on with adolescents.

When a teacher likes me they talk to me. A lot of teachers don't care and they ignore you if you pass them in the corridor. I try not to let teachers bring me down.

I have found that often teachers mainly focus on the louder, more open students. As quieter, shyer students, we are often just left to our own devices. We need the most help and have great ideas we could share with the class if given a chance.

If teachers encourage and have input into what I do, I want to do better and it's very encouraging. I definitely need encouraging. Some teachers put a lot of pressure on me. They say things are harder than they really are. I get really psyched out. It's hard to tell teachers things even if I trust them. They are authority figures.

From these comments we can see that the difference between a good teacher and a bad teacher has a lot to do with attitudes like confidence, trust and respect, and small kindnesses. Teachers have extraordinary potential to promote resilience in their young charges and help protect them from depression. We know from research that women who were sexually abused as children are more likely to cope as adults if they had a supportive, safe and respectful relationship with a teacher at some stage during high school.

However, teachers cannot be everything to students, least of all on their own. The challenges they face in their careers must be acknowledged—they need the backup and support of other teachers, the school principal, and the parent body at large.

Over the past decade, schools have become increasingly aware of the impact mental health problems such as anxiety and depression have on students and the broader school community. Many teachers want to know more about these problems and how they can support students experiencing difficulties. While professional development opportunities may be limited, there are websites that provide useful information and resources on supporting young people with mental health issues. Since 2000, *beyondblue: the national depression initiative*, has taken a leading role in raising community awareness about depression, anxiety, and related disorders and has information and resources about the impact of these problems on young people that can be accessed through its website: *www.beyondblue.org.au* and *www.youthbeyondblue.com*

Enhancing the social and emotional skills of students has some important pay-offs for the whole school community. Students with better social and emotional skills are more able to cope with the stressors of daily life, have better relationships with parents, teachers, and peers, and do better academically. Such skills also make it less likely that a student will experience a significant mental health problem in the future.

beyondblue has developed a curriculum program for junior secondary school students that teaches skills for managing the ongoing challenges of life (*www.beyondblue.org.au/schools*). The *beyondblue* classroom program is based on cognitive-behavioural principles (Chapter 11). This approach recognises that when an event happens to us, it is our thoughts and interpretations of that event, and not the event itself, that lead us to feel certain emotions and act in particular ways.

Thinking styles contribute to a person's vulnerability to experience mental health problems. Young people with negative thinking patterns about their selves, the world and their future are more vulnerable. The *beyondblue* schools classroom program was developed around six key senses. These are:

- **Sense of self-worth—the knowledge of and belief in one's strengths, skills and abilities—an acceptance of one's inherent value;**
- **Sense of belonging—the feeling of being valued, needed and accepted—being connected meaningfully to a social network;**
- **Sense of control—the belief that one has the skills and ability to cope with life challenges and to manage one's own emotions;**
- **Sense of purpose—the capacity to make sense of the world and to perceive some meaning in one's life;**
- **Sense of future—the hopefulness about the future, enabling us to act purposely and positively;**

- Sense of humour—being able to see the lighter and funnier side of life—including ones own foibles.

The importance of peers

Peers have a huge and obvious influence on teenagers' experience of school life and learning.

Why aren't my friends here when I need them? I write. I talk to my cat. I talk to my pillow—I abuse it, I yell at it and I tell it everything I wish I could say. I'm scared my friends will backstab me. They gossip if I don't act the way they want me to.

I look at other kids in my class. Some of them are really depressed because their parents have split up or died. One guy is in a wheelchair, a few are getting bullied because they are fat or different or something. Others do some pretty bad things at school and might be expelled. I don't have any real problems like this. I can do my work really well and I have some friends. But deep inside something feels really bad and I just keep quiet about it.

Life can be very complicated—relationships, peers, etc. I don't need unrealistic goals as well. A lot of the reason that kids leave school is related to drugs. They can't be bothered and they would rather do the drugs. A lot can't cope with the school work, and some don't bother turning up for exams. We can watch our friends destroying themselves and do nothing or we can offer help. But there is no point helping if we end up getting hurt ourselves. I tried to break away from my smoking friends. My other friendships made me strong enough to do this. Friendships split up because people are self-destructing and I have learnt to accept I can't do anything about it.

> After my father died suddenly last year from a stroke, I had to do many things to try to get back on track. Of course it still upsets me and I still miss him, but I have learnt to cope with it. I have found a group of friends that support me and care for me. I have learnt to cry when I need to. I have found activities like netball and singing help me cope. I have found that I enjoy my leadership role at school and being a role model to younger students. I have also learnt to talk to people about my problems.

Sometimes the behaviour of some of our children's friends makes us feel uneasy. Criticising them, however, or even keeping quiet about our concerns (our children often sense what we think, anyway) doesn't make it any easier to handle. The right time to express our views or take action might be when our teenager shares her concerns about a friend. If she remarks that she's really worried about her friend's smoking, we can talk with her about the problems of smoking, make clear what we think of it and support her wish to resist pressure to take up smoking herself.

Particularly in the vulnerable mid-teens, peer pressure competes with parent power and often wins. When asked what would most help him kick his drug habit, one boy replied, 'Get some new friends, I guess.' We are given precious few chances to play a significant role in our teenager's choice of friends, so it is important to tune in and show warm and sincere interest any time a teenager asks for help or advice in this regard.

School problems

As many as three in ten Australian students are thought to have academic or behavioural difficulties at school. The major concerns centre around poor performance, poor attendance and poor behaviour.

Poor performance

The reasons for underachievement may not be hard to find: bright kids may get bored and stop trying; some are turned off by what they see as irrelevant subjects; others fear their future employment prospects are bleak anyway and that 'learning this stuff' won't help; still others simply march to the beat of a different drum. Teenagers may do badly in subjects taught by teachers they don't like. But poor or deteriorating grades can also indicate emotional problems, specific learning difficulties or attention deficit hyperactivity disorder.

Emotional problems are the most common of all problems at school and should be suspected when a teenager is anxious, sad or angry about things that happen at home. Worry and stress short-circuit energy away from the task of learning, so falling marks can be a particularly sensitive indicator that something is amiss. Teasing by peers or teachers (see Chapter 9) and other hassles at school can also get young people down.

Specific learning difficulties should be suspected when there are particular problems with spelling, reading and mathematics, left/right confusion and a sort of absentminded professor approach to information. Around 15 per cent of students have significant learning or behavioural difficulties, and the earlier these are picked up the better.

Antisocial or aggressive behaviour, related mostly to frustration, can be a tip-off of learning difficulties, which are more common in boys. The two problems are often linked—learning problems can lead to behaviour problems and vice versa. Girls with learning difficulties experience frustration but are less likely to act it out, so their learning difficulties are more likely to go unnoticed and under-identified. Such teenagers may be reluctant to go to school or may develop some other form of anxiety.

What is ADHD?

Attention deficit hyperactivity disorder (ADHD, also ADD), was first described almost a century ago and is now recognised as an important cause of learning and behavioural difficulties. Few conditions and their treatment have created more controversy and confusion, although decades of research and experience have greatly improved our understanding. We know that ADHD is often hereditary and more common in boys than girls. Most affected children will have a close relative, usually male, with some features of the condition and more than half will carry some elements of the disorder into adulthood.

Everyone can summon up a picture of a hyperactive child: frenetic, disruptive, disorganised and infuriating. But most young people with the disorder have problems with impulsiveness and inattention as well as hyperactivity, and for some inattention is the main issue. The inattentive type, for obvious reasons, more often goes unrecognised. Because ADHD merges with the spectrum of normal behaviours there is no foolproof test for it. The three core behaviours—inattentiveness, impulsiveness and overactivity—are usually intense and pervasive, evident from the preschool years, and highlighted by the demands of school. Most children suffering from ADHD process new information slowly and have difficulty remembering the information they hear. As a result they find it difficult to follow instructions and complete tasks. For example, if asked to pack their school bag, they may remember only the 'Go to the kitchen and . . .' part and become distracted by the family dog along the way.

ADHD is usually diagnosed in childhood and its symptoms may become less severe by adolescence, but with the surge of hormones and all the other ups and downs, other problems can emerge and make it quite difficult to sort out. Even those who receive treatment can develop longstanding problems with self-worth and difficulty making friends. Some may get rebellious, while others become demoralised, anxious and depressed. These issues need to be addressed along with the ADHD.

If we suspect our child has ADHD, the local GP, community health centre or school counsellor can advise on tests. There is a bewildering array of suggested interventions, from medication to special education and behaviour support. Unfortunately, many alternative practitioners promote quick-fix, ineffective and expensive treatments such as spinal manipulation, mega vitamins, diet restrictions, eye exercises, tinted lenses and biofeedback.

The major controversies with ADHD/ADD have been over the prescription of stimulant drugs like Ritalin. Extensive research and clinical experience certainly show that medication given correctly is effective, particularly as part of a comprehensive package of help. Some teenagers are not too impressed with this pharmaceutical approach, however, like the fifteen-year-old girl who said, 'I tried Ritalin once. I could concentrate. It was boring.'

A boy with ADHD talked of his struggle with fears of rejection:

From Year 5 to 11 was the hardest time for me. At school, none of my friends knew that I had ADD and I didn't want them to know because I thought they might think differently of me and I thought they wouldn't want to be my friends any more. I didn't like taking tablets—they made me feel different—they changed my mood, my personality and I wasn't as talkative with my friends. But I found that everything was more organised. I was given heaps of help from teachers and tutors, but I hated it if my tutor was in the classroom with me. All the other students would know that she was there to help me. That made me feel really stupid.

One of the worst days was when one of my friends was searching my bag for food and he found my tablets. He told my friends and they all went quiet—I didn't like the way they reacted—it still hurts me to think about it. Then I changed schools but left the next school soon after.

While it can be reassuring to have a 'medical label', life's problems can rarely be traced to a sole organic cause or fixed with a single remedy. This is particularly true for teenagers and their families. Perhaps the two most practical things parents can do in this case are to join an ADHD support group (these can be found all over Australia and provide valuable information about services in your local area) and find out all they can about the condition.

Parents, and teachers too, can help by offering patience, praise and encouragement. Breaking tasks (such as getting dressed) into steps and, writing these down or drawing them can help a lot. So can reducing the amount of distraction and noise in the environment, particularly when you are trying to give instructions. Love, hugs, patience, understanding, one-on-one time, a balanced lifestyle and a positive focus are all the more important in nurturing teenagers with behavioural and learning disorders.

Poor attendance

Going to school can sometimes be a real drag, but for better or worse, secondary education has been compulsory in Australia for children under fifteen since World War II. The truant officer of old has been replaced by a network of people whose role is to find out why non-attenders are staying away and seek solutions in a friendly, supportive way.

Teenagers fail to attend school for a variety of reasons. If they are seriously ill or disabled, for example, they'll need time out to visit doctors or other health professionals or to be treated in hospital. Alternatively, parents may actually encourage them to stay at home to help out with the domestic chores or child care—not uncommon in families where education is not greatly valued.

Young people may also stay away from school with their parents' knowledge because the thought of going makes them anxious and distressed. Then there's truancy—an unauthorised absence from school that is usually concealed from parents. These two conditions are approached in different ways, and both need to be managed early by parents and schools.

School refusal

When a young person consistently says, 'I've got a headache' on school mornings but is perfectly well and happy on weekends, something's going on. If the doctor can't find a physical cause for these headaches—or tummy aches, or just feeling sick—it's all the more likely that we're looking at a case of school refusal. This complaint was once known as school phobia, and it can be accompanied by anxiety-related symptoms such as butterflies in the stomach, aching muscles, a racing heart, sweating, clammy hands, a lump in the throat, or shortness of breath. School-refusing teenagers may refuse to get dressed, leave the house or get in the car, so overwhelming may be their distress at the thought of facing school.

It may appear that a stressful situation or event at school is responsible, but in most cases the underlying problem is that the student doesn't want to leave home. Teenagers with this condition are often anxious about losing a parent, usually the mother; for them, staying at home is a way to keep tabs on her. Many school refusers are naturally anxious and afraid of new experiences. For example, if they had difficulty separating from their mother at preschool, they may develop school refusal at times of stressful change, such as moving up to primary school or from primary to high school.

About fifty per cent of such teenagers develop depression. School refusers are also at risk of continuing to suffer anxiety disorders, such as panic disorder and depression when adults. The parent involved may turn out to be anxious or depressed herself and holding onto the child out of her own psychological neediness.

School refusal can be treated; often this works best if parents also get advice and support (see Chapter 10). The most essential step is to take the teenager back to school gently but firmly, and as soon as possible.

Truancy

Truancy occurs when young people consciously 'wag' school in order to do something they regard as more enjoyable, such as playing in the park, seeing a movie or playing games at video arcades. Most of the kids who play truant do it with mates, just for the hell of it, hoping, of course, that no one finds out. Group pressure increases the risk that they will become involved in other problem behaviours such as stealing, graffiti, vandalism or drug abuse. A smaller group of truants are solitary individuals who have a serious mental health problem such as schizophrenia or an autism spectrum disorder.

Truancy can be dealt with by seeking support from teachers to keep attendance records and act promptly on absenteeism. Talking to the young person, giving respectful assistance with any learning difficulties, considering alternative subject choices and rewarding school attendance also help. So does giving truants more opportunities to feel they're contributing something at school. About one in five truants also suffers from depression; more rarely, they may have a psychosis or autism. In such cases it's essential to get professional help.

Some young people from minority cultures may feel alienated, misunderstood, threatened and discriminated against. School programs that strengthen cultural knowledge and build group cohesion and cooperation (for example, wilderness camps for indigenous Australians) help develop self-worth and also contribute to our multicultural society.

Other self-worth-building programs, like Reach, established by the charismatic footballer Jim Stynes in Victoria, and Father Chris Riley's Youth Off the Streets, bush school camps, or martial arts classes encourage both healthy independence and an ability to cooperate constructively with others. These types of activities can really help alienated, angry teenagers to get back on track. Unfortunately, many community activities that have traditionally fostered youth development, such as the netball and football teams, have disappeared, particularly from rural communities. Going to the pub or spending more time in cyberspace are not satisfactory substitutes for structured group activities that build social and cultural competence.

Truants are more likely to feel connected to school if they have someone to talk to and to trust, as one boy pointed out:

> I was given a hard time by other kids and teachers. I hated some subjects, had trouble taking tests and was worried about doing things in front of the class. Why wouldn't I want to leave school to do things I want to do? Then I left for a while and felt lost. A youth worker got me into an alternative school—I learnt to set some goals. I learnt that it's really up to me.

Poor behaviour

'Are teachers there to teach you or are they there to get you in trouble?' asked a girl in Year 7. This plaintive question raises an important point: What exactly is bad behaviour? Lack of attentiveness might just be the result of tiredness. Some kids are just not morning people, for example: it's very difficult for them to be bright-eyed and bushy-tailed at 8.30 am.

A pattern of aggressiveness or rebellion, on the other hand, is a worrying sign, especially when the teenager is doing badly in exams and assessments. Teenagers who consistently infringe the rights of others are extremely taxing to teach, often intimidating and ultimately destructive of school peace. It is worth noting that reports of violence in Australian schools are increasing.

Teachers and schools vary greatly in their handling of discipline problems. Fortunately, corporal punishment is no longer acceptable. The most effective techniques for controlling unruly kids involve setting out clear expectations for behaviour and rewarding those who meet them. Teachers also find it useful to sympathetically seek explanations for the misbehaviour and have a system of punishments such as demerits or loss of privileges. Other strategies are to suspend disruptive students from classes; keep them back after school hours; have them write out lines; or suspend and ultimately expel them from school—a drastic last resort. Many schools have a list of infractions and corresponding punishments so students at least know where they are on the trajectory to expulsion. But some take a more preventive view based on a whole-of-school culture, by fostering a sense of community, remembering to catch naughty kids doing something good now and then, and perhaps even inviting the student body to make the rules.

Some kids seem to be labelled as bad when there are clearly other factors at play. Teenagers who play up sometimes do so because they cannot see relevance in their studies, lose respect for education and become disenchanted with the authority of teachers.

There's another worrying thought. The people who do best in life are those who have self-confidence and feel good about themselves. These attributes are less likely to develop if the measures used to control students' behaviour involve fear, stress, uncertainty, confusion and failure. Enlightened schools know this and act accordingly.

Not all kids who play up at school need special education or punishment. As teachers well know, a class is made up of individuals with a wide range of abilities and personalities. In a given situation, it will be necessary to look closely at the young person causing concern in order to work out what is best. Does she just need tutoring or a change of school? Is he unwell? Is the poor behaviour due to a stress-related disorder, or are there other emotional problems involved for which he may need professional counselling? In most situations, the school should be able to point parents in the right direction.

Early school leavers

One in three teenagers leaves school each year without completing Year 12. Teenagers from lower socioeconomic backgrounds or isolated geographic areas are more likely to drop out of school early; only forty per cent of Aboriginal students stay at school until Year 10. Not surprisingly, those who hate school and did poorly in primary school are also likely to quit.

The disadvantages ahead for early leavers include higher unemployment rates (generally more than 20 per cent) and lower incomes than their high-school-graduate peers. They're also more likely to engage in vandalism and high-risk behaviours.

Early leavers asked for their views often say they'd like to see adult learning environments, where they will 'not be treated like two-year-olds', have an adult relationship with teachers, and be able to learn things directly related to their work goals. They want a meaningful education and chances to apply their learning.

What happens in the first year after leaving school is crucial. Getting full-time work reduces the risk of chronic unemployment, but it can be difficult for early leavers to get a job. The outcomes are better when vocational skills training taught by TAFE is offered to young people as a direct alternative to high school. This helps early leavers get jobs they could stick with, as well as boosting their productivity, which is good for our society as a whole.

The messages to remember

- A good teacher is long remembered, an inspiration for life.

- A sense of connectedness to school nurtures resilience in teenagers and is a major protective factor.

- By teaching young people to persevere and to solve problems at school, we help them gain skills for dealing with future adversity in life.

9
Stamping out bullying

Never be bullied to silence. Never allow yourself to be made a victim. Accept no one's definition of your life; define yourself.
—Harvey Fierstein

More than half of Australian students have been bullied at some time, and around one in six girls and one in five boys report being bullied at 'detrimental levels' once or more each week. Even more worrying, is the fact that intensive efforts to stop bullying appear to have failed.

The problem is a serious one. Bullying in childhood is linked to emotional problems in adolescence. It is associated with loneliness, poor academic achievement, sleep problems, headaches, bed-wetting, anxiety and depression, school refusal and trouble forming close friendships. In the long term, victims of bullying are more depressed and have lower self-esteem than teenagers who were never bullied.

Bullying occurs when someone hurts, threatens or frightens another person intentionally, repeatedly, without provocation. Bullying occurs in social groups, and there is an imbalance of power, whether real or perceived, between the bully and the victim.

Bullying can either be direct (openly confrontational) or indirect (the bully may hide behind someone else). It is also increasingly occurring via e-mail and the internet.

Physical bullying

- *Direct*: pushing, pulling, hitting or physically attacking someone; manhandling someone under the guise of horse-play; throwing things; using a weapon; damaging, removing or hiding another person's possessions without their permission.
- *Indirect*: Getting someone else to assault someone, remove or hide their belongings.

Verbal bullying

- *Direct*: Verbal insults or put-downs, name calling, teasing, ridiculing others and their achievements; verbally attacking someone about their race or religion; making physical threats or verbal demands including phone calls, notes, texts, emails; making sexual comments about another person.
- *Indirect*: Persuading a third party to insult someone else, spreading rumours, whispering about others in front of them.

Gestural bullying

- *Direct*: Glaring or making menacing or obscene gestures at another person.
- *Indirect*: Deliberately turning away, totally ignoring someone as if they don't exist.

Relational bullying

- *Direct*: Ganging up against someone, excluding people from the group, pressure to do things to join the group.
- *Indirect*: Persuading others to exclude someone, silent treatment, isolating or excluding someone.

Boys tend to bully both boys and girls and, as one might expect, are more involved than girls in physical bullying. Girls, on the other hand, tend to do their bullying indirectly, mainly bully other girls, and prefer verbal or silent treatment tactics. Bullying peaks in the early high-school years. The physical variety declines with age (as boys become a little less 'aggro', no doubt) while relational and indirect bullying continue or even increase through the high-school years. Nikki Goldstein of *GirlForce* magazine surveyed 5000 teenage girls about their friends. Eighty-seven per cent told her there was 'too much bitchiness at school' and 63 per cent reported being 'teased or bullied by their friends'.

For the victims, such experiences are distressing, isolating and unfair. Teenagers who are bullied have lower than average self-worth and are more inclined than others to stay away from school. Not only are victims of ongoing bullying likely to feel depressed and troubled, but sometimes the consequences are devastating—in some studies, a proportion of youth suicides is blamed on bullying. Contrary to the old rhyme, 'sticks and stones will break my bones but words will never hurt me', verbal and relational bullying are actually more likely to cause emotional harm and contribute to serious depression.

Bullies tend to be bigger than their victims or to band together in groups. Sensitive, shy, and introverted adolescents who overreact or underreact are common targets, as are those who are 'different', for example those who wear glasses or are overweight. Jeers of 'fatso' and the like in adolescence, by the way, appear to affect self-worth, body satisfaction and depressive symptoms well into the future. But any child or teenager can be bullied.

Why do children become bullies? Contrary to the stereotype, not all bullies come from broken homes or were especially aggressive as children. The reality is that family background, and number of parents in the home appear to have little bearing on who might become a bully. Similarly, some bullies are not angry but cool and well controlled. Bullies do place a high value on dominating other people and feel more respected because of their behaviour.

However, that doesn't mean they're winners. Being a bully is actually associated with higher levels of anxiety and depression, increased crime and anti-social behaviours and more referrals to psychological services. Those at particular risk are former victims turned bullies, who may be even more vulnerable to emotional disturbances than straight bullies or victims.

Bullying case histories

Joshua (victim) is small and thin and avoids the boisterous games in the playground or on sports days. He is a serious little kid who rarely if ever jokes in the classroom. He tends to give in to bullying peers in the hope they will then leave him alone, but he cannot hide his fear of them. Joshua's teacher describes him as anxious and extremely fearful about doing the wrong thing. He often feels flat and struggles to enjoy anything at school that involves his peers. He sees himself as unpopular and unable to fit in. The few friends he did have when he was younger now tend not to talk to him. Joshua says he feels extremely close to his family and spends most of his time outside school with them, but he has no really close friends. His mother is seen as very involved with his life and Joshua admits to being a little afraid of her when she is angry with him. She has struggled to accept that her son is bullied.

Mary (victim) doesn't smile much. She gives in quickly to bullies, who can readily sense her distress and fear. Both male and female peers have been known to bully her. The teacher describes her as anxious and almost too eager to do the right thing. She rarely seems to laugh or have fun, and looks sad when she thinks no one is watching. Mary sees herself as unpopular and feels that most of the other girls avoid her. She spends a lot of time worrying that her mother doesn't love her and may walk out on the family. Mary's mother finds it hard to believe that she is being bullied.

David (bully) is bigger than many other kids his age and enjoys boisterous, competitive games. He is one of the naughtier boys in class, struggling to focus. He sees himself as good-looking and popular. David admits to giving a few other kids a hard time both verbally and physically. These kids don't make him angry, but he can get things he wants from them, and it makes him feel good. His close mates do the same thing. David doesn't worry about his mean behaviour or how it might make others feel. He fights a lot with his siblings. His parents are harsh disciplinarians and 'everyone at home wants to be the boss'.

Ellen (bully) gets in trouble a bit in class. She sees herself as attractive and likeable. She gives a few of the other girls a hard time, usually by doing stuff behind their backs that leads to them feeling or being excluded. This is because either they have something she wants or it makes her feel good about herself. Her friends seem to happily join in. Ellen doesn't worry about this behaviour or how it makes others feel. Ellen describes her parents as very focused on being in charge. They are quick to punish her if she does something wrong.

Gary (bully-victim) is rated by classmates as the most likely to lose it in his class. He seems to just go off. Others, particularly bullies, can really wind him up. Then Gary takes a swing and gets in trouble while they look all innocent. He often gets teary and emotional when challenged about his behaviour by the teacher. When peers try to be nice to him he can react angrily and seems to want to fight. No one really likes him. Everyone has given up on trying to be nice. He finds school hard work and sees himself as a loser. Gary describes his family as distant and uncaring. He says he is able to outwit his parents and sometimes swears at them or slaps them. His parents are hard to predict when it comes to punishment: sometimes they come down hard and other times they don't seem to care. There is a lot of fighting at home.

Kate (bully-victim) seems to do her block regularly. Bullies are able to wind Kate up until she explodes. She often gets in trouble for retaliating and has got physical before. Kate gets very distressed, angry and teary when the teacher tries to manage her behaviour. When other kids have tried to be nice to her, she's bitten their heads off, so they have given up trying to be nice. No one really likes Kate. She finds school work difficult and sees herself as stupid, ugly and no good. She describes her family as lacking in warmth and affection: her parents are at a loss as to how to manage her and sometimes swear and hit her.

Bullying isn't only an issue between swaggering bossyboots and quaking victims. It depends on the support of many people: ringleaders, who organise a bullying group; followers; and reinforcers, who tend to applaud from a distance. In a given school group there are also likely to be outsiders who do not get involved—and defenders, who help the victim.

How can parents and schools help?

Given the seriousness of bullying for all concerned, we as parents have a particularly important role in picking up on it. Here are some things we can do:

- Keep an eye out for sudden changes in behaviour such as not wanting to go to school, spending a lot of time in the bedroom, a sudden disinterest in socialising, sudden anger at home, disappearance of friends, and lost or broken property.
- Acknowledge and accept what's happening and be careful not to minimise the experience—for victims in particular, this would be adding insult to injury.
- Don't rush in and try to rescue the situation with guns blazing; try talking with the teachers, principal or school counsellor to work out an effective approach. If school and parents get into conflict, the child falls un-helped through the gap.
- Do not approach the parents of the bully or try to mediate between the bully and victim. Let the school handle it.
- Teach the victim to relax, manage anxiety and be more assertive—and thus become a less attractive target. Build confidence and self-assurance by, for example, encouraging involvement in non-competitive sports and drama to build communication skills.
- Be on the lookout for signs of depression and arrange counselling for the victim or the bully or bully-victim as per the cases above; all three types have emotional problems.

- Become familiar with the school's anti-bullying policy
  or encourage the development of one if it doesn't
  already exist.

Most anti-bullying programs in schools fail because of a lack
of consistency in implementation. The more successful programs
reduce the numbers of students being victimised by teaching them
skills to protect and defend themselves.

A private boys' school in Sydney, Newington College, has done
this extremely well, dispelling myths about bullying and widely
publicising to students and parents the recommendations and
procedures for dealing with the problem. The policy includes
responses to the following common misconceptions:

- *I was just mucking around, can't he take a joke?* This
  is the most common response from the bully. In fact,
  bullying is not a joke. It is not funny to ridicule and
  hurt someone, to make them feel uncomfortable or to
  push them around.
- *I don't want to cause trouble.* This misconception
  comes from the victim, who thinks he is the cause of
  the problem. All students have a right to feel safe at
  school, and during their travel to and from school. You
  are only standing up for yourself when you report being
  bullied.
- *It is just a natural part of growing up.* This
  misconception comes from adults, but the truth is that
  there is nothing natural about being victimised.
- *No one can do anything about it.* Most cases of
  bullying are sorted out very simply, especially if the
  bullying is reported sooner rather than later. The
  school is committed to solving these sorts of problems,

but students must communicate with staff if the school
is to have any chance of helping.

- *Dobbing is a bad thing to do.* Bullying is the bad thing,
  telling the truth is a good thing. By telling the truth
  you are standing up for your rights as a human being.
  It takes character and intelligence to stand up for your
  rights, which is something that bullies are afraid of.
  Bullies try to intimidate people into maintaining a
  code of silence because they can then continue to hurt
  other people for as long as they wish. Bullying
  continues when people fail to report what is happening.

Young people can also take action on their own behalf

Concerned that bullying was widespread, Larissa Haywood and
other young people in the Holroyd Peer Education Project in
Sydney decided to do something about it themselves. They made
a DVD and a workshop guide using scenarios inspired by real-life
situations. *SPEAK OUT: Young People Against Bullying* outlines
what bullying is, the types of bullying, some of the reasons for it,
strategies to stop it, and where to go for help. The resource focuses
on the strategy of positive peer influence to stop bullying by putting
some of the responsibility for eliminating bullying in the hands of
the students and empowering and challenging them to change the
negative culture within their school or other environment. It notes
that bystanders can encourage bullies by their silence, as well as
by egging them on. Since it was launched in 2007 the resource
has been used by primary and secondary schools, youth services,
community organisations, local councils and parents.

Cyber bullying

The internet has opened up a new arena for bullies, who can
now harass and torment others via email, online chat rooms and

forums, and mobile phone services. Their methods include sending disturbing or threatening messages; posting offensive, defamatory or embarrassing photos and information; twisting what a person writes in chat rooms, spreading rumours or excluding them from chatting; and logging onto an online forum as someone else and causing mischief in their name. Cyber stalkers take things a step further by following a victim's movements around the internet, visiting the same chat rooms, leaving messages on message boards and sometimes encouraging a third party to engage in harassment. Cyber bullying is as common as it is nasty and dangerous.

More than two-thirds of Australian adolescents have attempted to conceal non-essential internet use from their parents; one in four have been bullied or harassed online; 17 per cent have used the 'report' button on MySpace; and over half do not know how to seek help.

Do's and don'ts when chatting (from the NSW Police)

- Don't ever give out the following information: your last name; your phone number (home or mobile); your private email address; your home address; what school you go to; sporting locations you attend; your parents' work location.
- Always be careful when entering information into a blog (it doesn't take too much to give your identity away); always check your chat profile to make sure that it doesn't include any personal information.
- Never email a picture of yourself to strangers or put a picture of yourself on your chat profile; never activate your webcam to persons you do not know in person or have just met on the internet; never show yourself naked in webcam videos or photos.

- Don't open up emails, files or web pages that you get from people you don't really know or trust; don't ever give out your password, except to responsible adults in your family; don't ever use a handle or nickname that may attract the wrong attention, eg 'sweet_teen', 'sexy_girl'.
- Remember: how people are in real life can be very different from how they are online—someone claiming to be a fifteen-year-old boy may be a fifty-year-old man! This is illustrated by the well-known cartoon of two dogs talking: 'I met someone wonderful in a chat room . . . and then I found out she's a cat.'

Although cyber bullying generally occurs outside school, schools can and do act against it. The single most effective intervention, as with the more traditional types of bullying, is having a whole school policy that spells out exactly how the problem is to be tackled. Schools can raise awareness and understanding by providing professional development for teachers, education sessions for parents and, ideally, frank discussions that involve teachers, parents and students.

Racism and prejudice

Unfortunately racism and cultural bigotry are also common among teenagers. These experiences of young people are heartbreaking:

> One day I overheard a fight between two boys at my school. It went like this: James yelled out, 'Scott, you are nothing but a stinking Abo.' Scott yelled back, 'No one's worse than an Abo.' And then they started laughing hysterically. I felt a tightness around my chest. I am Aboriginal. I have been called Abo, coon and boong. Words like that should be banned from the English language.

One of my friends thought that us Kooris got too much money from the government and wasted the money on alcohol and cigarettes. Fellow students make racist jokes and remarks just within ears' reach. The racism became even worse when a teacher, who thought she was making me feel important, was singling me out to ask if facts or events about Aboriginal history were correct.

I've always felt that I did not fit in anywhere and that people are just pretending. Kids at school say: 'You can't even tell that you are Aboriginal.' I was hurt on Sorry Day when friends said: 'Why do we have to say sorry to you? We didn't do anything wrong.'

Why do people carry negative preconceptions of something that they have not been exposed to? To take a stance on an issue they know nothing about? To judge a person not because of their personality but because of their physical appearance or race? Something happened today after school that really upset me. A man came into work and refused to be served by an 'Asian Gook'. What would possess a man who was probably himself a descendant of an immigrant or maybe even a convict to pass judgement on my racial background? How am I supposed to react to such ignorance? How am I going to cope if or when this sort of agonising encounter happens again?

And from a Muslim girl:

We are expected to be terrorists and to hate Westerners, yet we were born in Australia. People say things like, 'Where are you from?' We are perceived to be illiterate and uneducated. They think we don't have free rights, freedom of speech or equality with our men. They expect to hear we are forced to cover up and have arranged marriages. When we walk down the street, people call us threats to society and extremists.

It's easy to understand how young people subjected to such treatment could lose interest in school or even drop out. Martin Luther King wrote: 'In the end we will remember not the words of our enemies but the silence of our friends'. It is a powerful reminder for good people to be fiercely outspoken against racism.

The messages to remember

- Bullying is common and puts young people (bullies and victims alike) at risk of depression.

- Bullying is not natural, not unstoppable, and not the victim's fault.

- Bullying should always be reported and taken seriously. Schools can control bullying if bystanders report bullying and do not encourage it either by their silence or by egging the bully on.

- Teenagers involved in social networking via the internet tend to be too trusting and should be made aware of the dangers involved.

- Speak out about racism.

Part 3

How can we help adolescents overcome depression?

About one in five young people is experiencing significant psychological distress at any one time.

The vast majority of teenagers appear to sail through adolescence. In surveys, at least, around four out of five say that they are healthy, happy and satisfied with their lives. For about half of these kids, progress is smooth and for the other half it occurs in fits and starts. However, as we've seen, many teenagers don't fare so well. About one in five young people is experiencing significant psychological distress at any one time.

Some will overcome this distress and bounce back. Others may quietly or not so quietly self-destruct. Youth suicides and drug-related deaths have declined over the past decade, but the numbers of young people admitted to hospital after deliberately harming themselves or being diagnosed with emotional and behavioural problems have increased.

Helping young and vulnerable people comes down to understanding what is normal and what is abnormal, doing more to prevent problems, and intervening early and persevering if problems arise. As a general rule, if a teenager's behaviour changes suddenly, parents need to seek advice. But seeking outside help can be confronting, for both parents and teenagers, as this comment from a young woman shows:

> When I feel down, it helps if people make small gestures to show they understand. Things like: 'Get over it' or 'You need help' are not helpful.
>
> Some people are really good at hiding things and you don't really know they are in pain. A lot of people don't want to admit they've got a problem or that they're a head case. I wouldn't go to the school counsellor. I know he's there but I don't want anyone to know I'm seeing him. Sometimes it is easier to go to a total stranger.

In this section we look at:

- Steps to seeking help
- Challenging depressed thinking
- Antidepressant treatment
- Other mental and physical illnesses

10
Steps to seeking help

Alone we can do so little; together we can do so much.
—Helen Keller

E ven though depression is an illness that can be treated, many young people find it hard to ask for help or even assist their friends to do so because of the stigma attached to having a 'mental disorder'. One of the most important and helpful things that adults can say in such situations is, 'I don't always cope, myself.' Mental illness shouldn't be seen as something to be ashamed of. After all, the vast majority of people are touched by it at one time or another.

Above all, we must never underestimate the value of a caring parent, close friend, trusted teacher or student welfare coordinator— essentially, someone who listens. Our lives are shaped by the inner stories we tell ourselves about our experiences. We move away from 'thinking depressed' by retelling our stories to people we trust. When we do this, we learn to understand our experiences as challenges, not disasters.

People who have the courage to seek help will quickly discover a cruel fact: Australia has a shortage of specialist mental-health services for young people, though the tide may be turning as new initiatives gradually make a difference. Meanwhile, where does one turn?

Professionals who can help

A GP is in a good position to help parents. GPs understand the broad range of issues involved (for example, family relationships, mental health, drug abuse, sexual health) and how to access other help, and the cost is mostly, if not completely, covered by Medicare. Where there are concerns about confidentiality, the teenager may find it easier to see a GP who isn't the family doctor—preferably one with a special interest in adolescent health—to care for the young person while the parents attend the family doctor for support. Alternative sources of help include a teacher whom the teenager connects with and trusts, the counsellor or student welfare coordinator at school, a youth worker—often employed by the local council—a psychologist or a psychiatrist.

Respect for confidentiality is a crucial issue. Confidentiality means that 'Anything we discuss will be kept confidential', explains Dr Melissa Kang, a GP who works with adolescents.

That means that I will not repeat anything you tell me to anyone else, unless I think it would help you and you give me permission to do so. There are a few situations, however, where I will not be able to keep confidentiality, for example, if I am concerned that you could harm yourself or someone else, or that you are being harmed or at risk of being harmed because of somebody else and you are under sixteen. In these situations it would be my duty to ensure that you are safe. I would tell you if I need to notify somebody about something that you've told me and I would make sure that you have as much support as possible.

Young people often say it's the most important aspect of their relationship with a health professional or therapist. In fact, many teenagers will avoid seeking help if they believe their privacy might not be respected. When a professional promises confidentiality to an adolescent, she recognises that the young person is capable of exercising rational choice and giving informed consent. Even with teenagers under sixteen, the age of consent, common law recognises the concept of the mature minor. Confidentiality does not mean a young person won't be encouraged to confide in and seek support from their family and others who care about their wellbeing. However, although confidentiality is necessary so young people feel able to trust their health professional with sensitive information, sometimes their safety must take priority.

There is no fixed age at which a young person is deemed legally competent and therefore entitled to confidentiality. The degree of understanding and judgement will differ from teenager to teenager.

Using the health-care system: a young person's guide

Even when parents know to contact a GP in cases of family distress, it is important for young people to know how to choose and visit a GP on their own, because they often keep their distress to themselves. They should be given the following basic information.

To make an appointment with the doctor of your choice, phone or drop in and ask the receptionist for:

- a long appointment if discussing the problem will take longer than fifteen minutes
- an urgent appointment if the problem is urgent, although it's better to try to make an appointment before the problem becomes a crisis

If you need to visit a doctor and you don't have a **Medicare card**, the receptionist will take your name and call the Medicare hotline to get your parent's or guardian's Medicare number. If you are unable to pay, you can ask the doctor or the receptionist if it is possible to sign a bulk billing form. This means that Medicare pays the full cost of your visit to the doctor and a bill will not be sent to your parents.

If you are sixteen or over, you can have your own Medicare card. All you need to do is visit your local Medicare office with identification such as a birth certificate and fill in a Medicare enrolment form. If you don't have any identification, you can give your parent's or guardian's name. Your name will then be taken off your parent's card and you will get your own card. This card will be sent to you in the mail. When visiting your doctor, remember to take your Medicare card. For more information, contact the Medicare hotline on 132011. If you have any problems with these procedures, ask your doctor or the receptionist.

If you are receiving or about to receive benefits from Centrelink, you will instantly get a **Health Care Card**. If you are under sixteen and your parents have a Health Care Card, then you can use their card. If you don't live at home, you may be entitled to the youth homeless allowance from Centrelink. It is helpful to see a social worker to determine if you are eligible to seek this allowance. If you are over sixteen and earn less than a certain amount, you may qualify for a Health Care Card. Visit your Centrelink office with some identification and staff will help you fill in an application form. A Health Care Card has many benefits, such as cheaper health care, cheaper medicines and travel concessions.

Note: GPs can access the *Adolescent Health GP Resource Kit, 2nd Edition* which contains helpful information on dealing with adolescents (*www.caah.chw.edu.au*)

The messages to remember

- Important sources of support include school-based counsellors, nurses or pastoral care staff, youth workers linked to local Councils or community centres, GPs, psychologists, psychiatrists or other therapists.

- In seeking help or treatment for a teenager in emotional or physical distress, the GP is often the most appropriate first port of call.

- Reassurance about confidentiality is very important to adolescents. It's a good idea for young people to know how to visit a doctor on their own if need be, preferably before a crisis arises.

11
Challenging depressed thinking

Change your thoughts and you change your world.
—Norman Vincent Peale

As we've seen, there is a lot we can do to help teenagers overcome depression. The first thing is to find a trustworthy non-judgemental therapist who can help the young person understand the problem and develop hope. The most effective proven treatment for adolescent depression is *cognitive behavioural therapy* (CBT). The idea behind CBT is that thoughts, feelings and actions are connected. When an event happens to us, it is our thoughts and interpretations of that event, not the event itself, that lead us to feel certain emotions and act in particular ways.

Depression tends to build in a spiral. For example, a depressed teenager may not feel like talking to his friends, who may then leave him out of things. This makes him even more depressed. Depression leads to negative experiences, which lead to even more depressed feelings. CBT aims to reverse this downward spiral through:

- *adaptive thinking* as a counter to negative thought patterns

- *social training and modelling* to teach helpful, successful behaviours
- *desensitisation* to help us relax, and weaken the hold of depressed thoughts
- *reinforcement* to encourage healthy behaviour and helpful thinking patterns

After eight to twelve sessions of CBT, depressed young people usually start feeling better. These sessions may be one on one or, less commonly, in a group with other young people. It can be very helpful for the teenager's parents to attend some of the sessions so they can learn about depression and the nature of the treatment in order to provide support. Parents can also receive help for any emotional problems, including depression, which they may be experiencing.

CBT usually involves seeing a therapist, who may be a GP, psychologist or psychiatrist with specific training. However, some young people with depression and anxiety are helped by completing a program of CBT online. This is called e-therapy and may include connecting with a therapist via email or telephone. Obviously, this form of CBT is ideal for young people who live in rural or remote areas, or where there is no therapist locally available to provide help. An example of an online approach to the treatment of depression by the Australian National University can be seen at *www.moodgym.anu.edu.au* or *www.ecouch.anu.edu.au*.

Here is some information about techniques in cognitive behavioural therapy.[1]

Changing thought patterns

We human beings have around 40 000 to 60 000 separate thoughts per day. The vast majority are old thoughts that are stored in the subconscious. Some of these are negative, *pessimistic thoughts*. For example, we may believe deep down that: 'I must be good at everything in order to feel worthwhile.' CBT asks that we gently question the evidence for such beliefs and consider whether they are helping or not. What would happen if we changed our thinking? Through this process, we might arrive at the more helpful thought, 'It's OK to make mistakes.' Here are some examples of unhelpful thinking patterns:

Black-and-white thinking supposes that things are either awful or perfect. For example, students may focus totally on one goal, like 'getting into university'. This predisposes them to feeling like a failure if their only choice doesn't eventuate. The common belief that 'good things happen to good people' and 'bad things happen to bad people' (perpetuated in many cartoon shows and fairy tales) sets young people up to think that something must be wrong with them if things go badly. CBT asks us to think about shades of grey and try to become aware of the feelings and thoughts in between the extremes.

Common negative *over-generalisations* include thoughts such as 'I can't do anything,' 'I'm a lazy person,' and 'Nobody likes me'. The evidence for these unhelpful thoughts needs to be challenged with self-questioning along the lines of, 'What are my strengths?' and 'What are the things I'm proud of?'

Mind-reading involves making assumptions about what someone else thinks of us or believes about us. In CBT, the evidence for such assumptions is questioned, for example, 'How do you know this?', 'How can you be sure?', 'Might your friend have something else on their mind?'

Making mountains out of molehills is a tendency to exaggerate and to say things like, 'It will be awful, terrible, horrible' and, 'I can't stand it any more'. With CBT, we're prompted to examine how this catastrophic type of thinking makes us feel, and to find a more helpful approach, such as: 'Yes, It will be difficult, but I have got through such things before and I will try to do my best.'

Wasting time worrying speaks for itself. The challenge here is to focus on things we can do something about, rather than on things over which we have no control. CBT aims to teach a young person to practise 'coping' thoughts, before, during and after a stressful situation such as an exam, something like, 'This is going to be hard but I know how to deal with it.' After the exam, positive thoughts may be reinforced with statements like 'I'm doing better at this all the time,' 'I handled that well.'

It can also help to keep a diary record of all the unhelpful and helpful thoughts that tend to arise—what we really think and feel in certain uncomfortable or stressful situations. This helps us monitor progress, identify short-term and long-term goals, and become more focused.

Helpful ways of thinking about difficult situations

- Mistakes are part of learning and growing.
- It's normal to feel a little up and down.
- It's normal for things to go wrong.
- What is the worst thing that can happen?
- Will it matter in a few months?
- Difficult situations can help me become stronger.
- It's OK to ask for support.
- I am getting to know myself.
- I can be myself, not what others expect me to be.
- I can change.
- I respect and accept myself.
- I am a unique person.

> **Helpful questions to challenge unhelpful thinking**
> - How would I help a friend if he/she were in this situation?
> - Is there another way to think about things?
> - Why am I thinking like this? What are the reasons?
> - What is the argument in my head?
> - Are these thoughts useful or helpful?
> - How are my thoughts making me feel?
> - Is there a more helpful way to think about things?

Social skills

Many depressed young people find it hard to make and keep friendships, and even to socialise. This makes them feel isolated—which only deepens their depression. In CBT, a teenager will be asked whether or not she feels confident with:

- **Big skills.** These include taking turns, sharing, apologising, owning up, expressing feelings, giving compliments, receiving compliments, gaining attention in positive ways, listening to others, communicating, dealing with arguments, negotiating compromise, saying 'hello' and 'goodbye', giving and accepting criticism, asking for help, offering help, joining in, inviting others, acting confidently, saying 'no' when appropriate, standing up for yourself, and dealing with bullying.
- **Small skills.** These include maintaining good posture, saying enough in conversations, making eye contact, using appropriate facial expression, voice volume and tone, head movements (for example, nods), body movements (for example, fidgeting), and expressive gestures, and gauging and keeping a proper social distance.

A therapist can help the young person identify problems with big and small skills. Practising social skills in daily life can help improve the skill and create confidence.

Making friends

Most of us like to be noticed. If a teenager doesn't have people noticing him sometimes, he feels invisible and as if he doesn't belong. There are good and bad ways to be noticed. CBT prompts young people to consider which ones they use and which ones other teenagers they like and respect use. For example, showing an interest in other people is a good way to be noticed, but showing off or making nasty or sarcastic comments are bad ways to be noticed.

If young people use bad ways to be noticed, they will still be noticed, of course—it's hard for other people *not* to notice this sort of behaviour. CBT invites them to reflect on whether being hurtful or making others feel bad actually makes others like them and whether such behaviour really suggests they don't like themselves very much.

It may be worth talking with your teenager about what being a friend—as distinct from 'a kid I see at school'—means to them and what qualities they seek in a friend. Here is what teenagers say about the characteristics of a good friend: understanding, caring, honest; loyal even when under peer pressure not to be; accepts you for who you are; lets you be yourself and is not judgemental; will still like you even if they disagree with you; you can talk to them about anything; is there in good and bad times.

Calming the body and mind

Depressed people often forget to seek out and do pleasant things, which is why they often complain of boredom. In CBT, the young person is asked to plan simple, pleasurable things to do every day and to write them down in a diary. 'Pleasant things could include breathing clean air, feeling the sun on your back, punching a bag, bongo drumming, lying on the ground and looking at the clouds, playing sport or reading, listening to music, talking to an old friend or making a new one, laughing, singing, taking a bath, dancing, playing a musical instrument, eating chocolate. It may be helpful to ask: 'When you are happier, what do you find yourself doing?'

All these activities are not only pleasing to the senses but also relaxing. Specific exercises in mindfulness, breathing, muscle relaxation and visualisation can also help increase teenagers' sense of peace and inner harmony. Routes to relaxation are many, and include massage, exercise, meditation, prayer, hypnosis and yoga. Whichever method is chosen, practising relaxation every day for as little as five to ten minutes leads to a lower heart rate and blood pressure and greater resilience and resistance to stress. Here are some practical exercises to try every day.

Mindfulness

Mindfulness is a relaxed state of mind. Try to watch your thoughts as an observer. Don't try to stop stressful thoughts but allow them to flow through your mind and observe them from a distance. Sometimes the statement, 'just relax', can make things worse because your active mind finds it difficult to stop thinking and worrying. Instead, accept your active mind and step aside from your thoughts. Let your thoughts just flow through your mind.

Breathing exercise

This is an easy exercise to do at school or before any stressful task. To learn the technique, sit comfortably in a quiet room. Count how many complete breaths you take in sixty seconds. Then breathe in for a slow count of three (one . . . two . . . three . . .) and out for a slow count of three, for a full minute. Try counting your breaths over sixty seconds again and compare the total to what it was before the exercise. The breathing rate often slows down, which in turn helps the heart slow down and the whole body relax.

Muscle relaxation

Lie down on your back or sit in a comfortable chair. Become aware of the muscle groups in your body: your hands, arms, shoulders, jaw, face and nose, stomach and legs and feet. Tense your muscle groups for a few seconds and then let them go as follows.

Hands: Make a fist with each hand and let go and relax.

Arms: Stretch your arms out in front of you, raise them high up over your head and stretch higher. Let your arms drop back to your side and feel them go floppy.

Shoulders: Pull your shoulders up to your ears. Hold in tight and then relax.

Jaw: Clench your teeth together really hard. Then let your jaw hang loose.

Face and nose: Make lots of wrinkles on your forehead, and crinkle up your nose, then let your face go smooth.

Stomach: Pull your stomach in. Make it touch your backbone. Get as skinny as you can, then release your stomach.

Legs and feet: Push your feet and toes down on the floor. Let your feet and toes go loose and floppy.

Take time to let each muscle group lose the tension and relax.

Visualisation

Visualisation of past pleasant experiences is a powerful way to instant relaxation. Think of one of your favourite places, like the beach, a bush walk, a garden or a park. Imagine the smells, sounds, touch and scenery. Bring yourself back to the state of your mind when you were last at this place. Try to feel a wonderful state of quietness and peace in this place. Feel a sense of contentment. Take a deep breath in and out.

Communication

As we've seen, depressed adolescents often feel isolated. Talking about their problems and concerns in a positive way can help enormously by enabling them to express themselves and ease their sense of isolation.

For parents, it's important to listen. We can use eye contact and other body language to show that we're paying full attention. When our teenager states what the problem is, it can help to restate it in our own words: 'It sounds as though . . .'; 'Let's see if I understand what you are saying . . .'. This approach demonstrates that we have truly heard the meaning of what is being communicated. It is not about agreeing or disagreeing. It is about communicating that we have listened fully.

CBT encourages young people to focus on the issue at hand rather than 'everything all at once', and to use positive expressions like 'I feel . . .' rather than 'you make me . . .' and other forms of blaming and accusation. Parents can help by taking this approach too. We can also avoid interrupting, over-generalisations such as 'you always', 'you never', lecturing, using a sarcastic tone or bringing up the past. It's also good to keep statements brief, use a neutral tone and practise relaxation ourselves.

Teenagers learn their communication style at home as well as from friends. Common approaches that end by reducing communication, not improving it, include: talking through a third person (for example, 'Mum told me that she heard you missed school today'), accusing, blaming, threatening, making defensive statements, interrupting, over-generalising, making extreme, rigid statements such as 'You never do any homework', lecturing, preaching, getting off the topic, commanding, dwelling on the past (for example, 'You used to be such a nice happy toddler, now you're always miserable'), monopolising the conversation, remaining silent or not responding when spoken to.

Alternative, more helpful, communication styles include: talking directly to the person involved, making 'I' statements like 'I feel', listening, making sure our statements of fact are accurate, making brief problem statements, using 'I would like' statements (for example, 'I heard from your teacher that you had to leave school on two afternoons last week. I would like to talk about that and help if I can'), sticking to the present issue, using clear and simple language, suggesting alternative solutions, and validating concerns.

Problem solving

Depressed teenagers lose their ability to solve problems and think their way out of difficulty. This makes them feel even more useless and hopeless. Therapists assist young people to define their problems, and then brainstorm solutions and their likely outcomes. These solutions are written down in a diary or on a whiteboard. Young people are encouraged to put them into action and report back at the next session.

Here are some helpful problem-solving questions:

- What effect is the problem having on my life?
- Imagine my problem has been solved. How would I feel?
- How would I know it had been solved?
- What changes would I notice?
- What steps could I take to make these changes?
- What needs to change?
- What changes would I like to see in my life? What are my goals?

Other psychological treatments

Several other types of psychotherapy may be of help to depressed adolescents.

Interpersonal therapy (IPT) focuses on developing insight into social and relationship problems that may be contributing to the depression, and finding solutions for them. IPT emerged from Freudian psychotherapy.

Therapists are empathetic and help the patient reflect on their feelings and experience and how these might be linked to earlier relationships, such as with a parent. The therapy might focus on grief over a death, conflicts and disputes with family members, or adjusting to a new role, for example, becoming aware that one is gay or lesbian. IPT is an effective treatment for depression in adults and there's growing evidence that it can also help teenagers. Parents may also be taught about depression so they can support their child in the therapy.

In **family therapy**, everyone in the family regularly meets with a therapist with the aim of improving communication, resolving conflict, and changing patterns of family interaction that might contribute to depression, anxiety and low self-esteem. There is an overlap between some forms of family therapy and CBT or IPT involving the parents.

Young people have a better chance of recovering from depression if their parents and family understand the nature of depression and its symptoms, support their treatment and are able to improve communication and problem-solving within the family. If a parent herself suffers from depression or anxiety or another mental illness, the teenager will recover more completely if the parent too receives appropriate treatment.

Dealing with physical symptoms

When a teenager presents with aches and pains (headache and abdominal pain are the most common), tiredness and lethargy or vague feelings of ill-health, and the doctor has ruled out physical causes, this is called *body mind syndrome*. Sometimes the sufferer reports more serious changes, like losing function or sensation in a limb or having difficulty walking. Many different labels have been given to these presentations such as psychosomatic disorder or somatising syndrome but they share some basic characteristics:

- *The symptoms are overvalued*, that is, the sufferer is preoccupied with them beyond what one would expect. For example, a teenager with headaches who is well but finds it hard to think about anything but the next headache.
- *The symptoms are out of proportion to the physical findings*. A doctor can find no adequate evidence to account for the degree of discomfort or disability.
- *The symptoms are enduring and distressing*, not minor or occasional complaints, like a momentary twinge.

In such cases, a frustrating medical merry-go-round in search of a 'respectable disease' will not provide the answer. The challenge is to understand what the illness might be telling us, validate the suffering involved and take a positive view of the likelihood of recovery, which, for a teenager, is almost inevitable if the adults around her express confidence about this! It is very powerful when people say, 'You are going to get through this,' 'You are going to be OK'.

Tiredness and fatigue are common symptoms of depression and anxiety in young people and a major aspect of *chronic fatigue syndrome*. Psychological fatigue often presents as a feeling of weariness associated with loss of motivation and interest and loss of a normal sense of pleasure. It characteristically fluctuates with mood and improves with activity. This is why exercise is so therapeutic for anyone who has depression or any other mental illness.

The messages to remember

- A good therapist, who is kind, accessible and non-judgemental, can help a young person understand their problem, develop hope, and experience some success in overcoming their difficulties.

- A form of psychological therapy called cognitive behavioural therapy (CBT), based on the idea that *thoughts, feelings and actions are connected*, is the most effective proven treatment for adolescent depression.

- Parents can be usefully and effectively involved in helping their adolescents overcome depression through listening, support, encouragement, facilitating access to services and encouraging involvement in pleasant activities.

12
Antidepressant treatment

If you want others to be happy, practise compassion. If you want to be happy, practise compassion.
—The Dalai Lama

Antidepressant medication tends to be used for teenagers who are lost in their depression and have failed to respond to CBT. Levels of serotonin, an important chemical in the brain, have been linked with depression. The antidepressants of choice are *selective serotonin reuptake inhibitors* (SSRIs), which may help restore normal levels of serotonin in the brain and relieve feelings of depression.

The most frequently experienced side effects of an SSRI, particularly at the beginning of treatment, are nausea, headaches and diarrhoea. These symptoms usually disappear within a week to ten days. Sometimes they're less bothersome if the medication is taken with food or paracetamol or if the tablets are taken at a different time of the day. Antidepressants are prescribed only by doctors and work best when the patient has had some advice about depression and the possible side effects of the medication, and receives regular reviews and sympathetic counselling.

Are antidepressants safe for young people?

On the one hand, youth depression is increasingly prevalent and often under-detected and under-treated, and we know untreated depression can be harmful. On the other hand, community concern is growing about an increase in the prescribing of antidepressants by GPs and reports that SSRIs may precipitate suicidal behaviour in adolescents.

In Australia, none of the SSRIs is approved for the treatment of depression in adolescents. SSRIs are approved by the Therapeutic Goods Administration only for the treatment of Obsessive Compulsive Disorder (OCD) in young people. However, in light of an evaluation by the UK Committee on Safety and Medicines, the Australian Adverse Drug Reactions Advisory Committee (ADRAC) released three recommendations for the treatment of depression with SSRIs in 2004:

- **Any SSRI use in adolescents with severe depression should be undertaken only within the context of comprehensive management of the patient. Such management should include careful monitoring for the emergence of suicidal ideation and behaviour, especially with dose adjustment.**
- **The choice of SSRI for adolescents should be made taking into account the recent evaluations of clinical trial data and product information.**
- **Adolescents who are currently being treated for major depression with an SSRI should not have their medication ceased abruptly.**

beyondblue: the national depression initiative, provided the following guidelines in 2004:

- It is essential that patients and their carers are given sufficient information regarding the risks and benefits associated with these medications to enable them to make an informed decision.
- Treatment needs to be tailored to the individual based on a comprehensive assessment of the young person, their family and social circumstances, and issues of risk.
- Given the possible increased risk of suicide, doctors, patients and their carers should observe for warning symptoms including increased irritability, impulsiveness, agitation, restlessness, reckless behaviour, or overt suicidal thoughts and self-harming actions.
- Patients and carers need clear information about what to do in a crisis situation or emergency.
- Close, regular review is essential when starting treatment and with dosage adjustments (up or down).

Having brief depression-symptom checklists that the teenager and his parents complete each day is useful. It can be discussed by all of them, and the doctor, at the regular review. Understanding what side-effects may occur helps ensure the teenager feels less anxious if he experiences any symptoms and is more likely to cooperate with treatment.

It's not certain exactly how long a young person should continue to take an antidepressant after she has recovered. If the depression has been severe and it has taken two to three months to recover, then it's recommended that she continue the medication for twelve months. Adults who have experienced repeated episodes of depression are more likely to remain well if they continue to take the antidepressant. After all, people with conditions such as high blood pressure remain well on long-term medication. Depression, which occasionally can be a chronic and recurring condition of the brain, may be regarded in the same way.

As part of their treatment, young people who suffer from depression need to learn that it may be in their nature to become depressed again. They should understand that the regular use of medication and the psychological techniques learned in CBT might be essential to maintaining their mental health.

The messages to remember

- When teenagers are lost in their depression and have failed to respond to CBT, a doctor (and only a doctor) may recommend antidepressant medication.

- Be patient. The medication may take a few weeks to drive away the depression.

- Antidepressants work best in combination with education about depression, with regular reviews and with sympathetic counselling.

- Side effects can occur but will generally settle down. All medications have adverse side effects and in rare cases, antidepressants may be associated with an increase in aggressive behaviour and suicidal thoughts. These symptoms must be reported immediately to the prescribing doctor.

- You can't become hooked on antidepressants. They are not addictive.

13
Other mental illnesses

Health is always present regardless of the presence
of disease, as the skies are present in spite of
clouds on the horizon.

—Norman Sartorius

D epression is sometimes associated with other mental illnesses or disorders. These conditions may begin as a depression of mood, but the young person then becomes clearly more unwell with new symptoms, and the usual approaches to treatment of the depression do not lead to recovery. Conversely, the teenager may already have an anxiety disorder or ADHD and may subsequently develop depression as well. The assessment and treatment of teenagers with these more complicated problems usually require the help of a child and adolescent psychiatrist.

Conditions commonly associated with depression are: a range of anxiety disorders including obsessive-compulsive disorder, post-traumatic stress disorder, eating disorders such as anorexia nervosa and bulimia, bipolar disorder and schizophrenia.

Anxiety—more than a racing heart

Anxiety is normal and, in small bursts—for example, just before exams or that big race—it can be helpful. But overwhelming and persistent anxiety seriously interferes with a young person's life.

The signs of anxiety include restlessness, irritability, muscle tension, poor concentration, physical symptoms such as palpitations or 'butterflies in the stomach', disturbed sleep and fatigue or tiredness. If these symptoms persist and interfere with the young person's daily life, he or she is likely to have an anxiety disorder.

Anxiety disorders come in a variety of forms. When a young person is generally over-anxious, constantly experiencing the symptoms of anxiety, she is said to have *generalised anxiety disorder*. Alternatively, if she only becomes anxious when separated from her parents and home environment, she may have what is called *separation anxiety disorder*. In teenagers, separation anxiety and school refusal (see Chapter 8) are often associated with a depressive illness.

An anxiety disorder might also develop following a stressful life event such as the break-up of the parents' marriage or serious illness in a family member. These reactions usually settle when the source of stress is resolved.

Some older adolescents develop intense fear associated with physical symptoms such as sweating, choking and chest pain and believe that they might lose control or even die. When these distressing *panic attacks* (see Appendix, pp. 193–4) occur in specific locations, such as shopping centres, the individual may come to avoid these places, a condition called *agoraphobia*.

A number of young people have excessive and persistent fears or phobias about certain objects or situations. In younger children phobias are more likely to be straightforward and relate to tangible things, but in teenagers they may become more complex and relate to events such as visiting the doctor or meeting people socially.

Obsessive compulsive disorder is a form of severe anxiety in which the young person has intrusive, repeated thoughts and impulses which they try to control by repetitive behaviours or compulsions such as hand washing or checking the door is locked. The young person is driven to undertake these actions according to some self-imposed rule. He then becomes anxious that the act was not done correctly and is driven to perform it again. Such rituals consume increasing amounts of the young person's time.

Treatment of anxiety disorders

All of these anxiety disorders require treatment and counselling. Fortunately, most respond well to psychological treatment, particularly cognitive behavioural therapy. Sometimes antidepressants which also reduce anxiety may be prescribed.

Education of parents about the nature of anxiety and helping them manage any anxiety of their own, effectively manage their children's behaviour and resolve family conflicts, can all contribute to the young person's recovery.

An anxious girl

Susan, a thirteen-year-old girl, was taken to see the family GP on the insistence of the school teacher. Over the past year, Susan had been rarely at school and when present, was uncooperative, interrupted the other students and had once tried to hit her teacher when reprimanded for refusing to do some work. She had frequently been brought to the GP by her mother because of recurrent abdominal pain with no clear cause and referrals to a specialist surgeon and a gynaecologist were planned.

Susan felt a sense of panic when faced with the prospect of getting up and getting ready for school. When at school she constantly felt anxious and was worried that 'something dreadful might happen to her mother'. She experienced difficulty falling asleep, needed to have the light on and would often wake up feeling fearful. Even when Susan was allowed to stay home from school, she still felt sad and grumpy, although she was helpful with housework, cared for her 15-month-old sister and also completed some of the school work that her teacher had sent home.

It emerged that Susan's mother had become increasingly depressed following the birth of her youngest daughter. She was withdrawn, felt anxious, sad and irritable, was unable to leave the house, spent long periods of time in bed and sometimes felt suicidal. On one occasion, when Susan discovered that her mother had taken some extra sleeping tablets during the day and was hard to rouse, she called her father at work. No medical assistance was sought for this episode, but her mother did indicate to Susan later that, at the time, she had wished to die.

Clearly, Susan had become anxious about her mother's mental health. She was not so much fearful of attending school, but of leaving home where she felt she needed to stay to keep her mother safe and to care for her younger sister. The management in this case involved treatment of the mother's *postnatal depression*, education and involvement of the father in support of the family and some counselling for Susan. Once Susan was confident that her mother was being properly cared for, she recovered from her anxious, depressive and somatic symptoms and happily returned to school. The teacher modified her school program so that she could catch up with her peers and not experience failure.

Post-traumatic stress disorder

Some adolescents may experience an extremely distressing and uncontrollable event in which their life, personal safety and security are threatened: a bad car crash, a deadly fire, being kidnapped, raped or witnessing the death of loved ones. Even after the event is over and they are safe and secure, they may be haunted by fear, anxiety, and recurring thoughts and dreams about what happened. They may develop feelings of detachment, or behavioural problems such as irritability, sleep difficulties and feelings of tension.

For most young people, these understandable reactions settle over several weeks. But for some, they persist. Young people who have experienced sexual abuse are particularly at risk in this regard, and females are more vulnerable than males.

If a young person continues to have disabling mental health problems after a trauma, she may have *post-traumatic stress disorder*. Such teenagers are in need of specialised help.

Eating disorders

While the causes of eating disorders are complex, social pressures are thought to play a part. In women's magazines over the past twenty years or so, articles about dieting have increased more than threefold. An American study noted that the women in *Playboy* centrefolds have become progressively thinner over time. Impossibly thin mannequins are used to display clothes in fashion stores. Wherever girls look, they get the message that thin is in.

In the late 1990s some 70 per cent of girls aged ten to eighteen told researchers that photos in fashion magazines influenced their idea of the perfect body shape. Nearly half reported wanting to lose weight because of such pictures. Now, cult websites are popping up promoting anorexia as a desirable lifestyle rather than the serious disease it is. These sites are aimed at—and tended by—girls between the mid-teens and mid-twenties. On one site, the following reasons not to eat were posted:

- 'You will be FAT if you eat today. Just put it off one more day, hour, minute and second.'
- 'People will remember you as 'the beautiful thin one', not 'the ugly fat one!'

- 'Bones are clean and pure. Fat is dirty and hangs on your bones like a parasite.'
- 'When you start to get dizzy and weak you're almost there.'

In the process of compiling her illuminating book *Ophelia Speaks*, author Sara Shandler reviewed over 800 contributions from adolescent girls, revealing the key concerns in their lives. She noted that the single most written-about subject was eating disorders: 'In the world of adolescent girls, thinness—sometimes at whatever cost—evokes profound jealousy. We lust for the perfect body. Even when we publicly condemn those who "control" their food intake, many of us privately admire their "willpower".'

Around 10 per cent of Australian females are believed to have some sort of eating disorder and an even greater proportion are obsessed with their body image. And the problem starts appallingly early: more than half of all twelve-year-olds want to be thinner. Associate Professor Jennifer O'Dea, a body image expert at the University of Sydney, surveyed 9000 young people across the country in 2006, and found that 42 per cent of high-school girls were dieting and 27 per cent thought they were too fat.

Eating disorders are most common in adolescent girls, and their onset is a distress call. The essential ingredient in anorexia, from the individual's point of view, is a struggle for personal control. Psychologically, anorexics seemingly do not want to grow up, while bulimics, who are usually older, do not handle being grown up too well. Both groups share a fear of weight gain, feelings of ineffectiveness, and low self-worth.

Anorexia nervosa is the third most common chronic disorder in adolescents, after obesity and asthma. It is a condition in which sufferers refuse to maintain a minimal, normal weight.

Anorexia nervosa typically occurs in a high-achieving and previously well-adjusted child. It may start insidiously, often after a chance remark about weight or fatness, but the end result is that dieting gets out of control. It's fairly easy to tell that something's wrong. Apart from the fact that your teenager looks underweight, she may insist she's fat no matter how thin she's become; say she has a sense of control when she says 'no' to food; avoid eating with the family or go straight to the bathroom after eating to throw up; get hooked on exercise; and stop having periods.

Anorexia is a dangerous illness, but treatment exists and recovery is possible. A beautiful young woman who was seriously malnourished and suicidal was hospitalised with anorexia nervosa when she was sixteen. Two years later she wrote an account of her successful treatment, which concluded:

> Today I am no longer worried about my weight. I control my life through other means by making sure I eat, sleep and study at specific times . . . All that matters today is that I am a normal, happy and healthy girl with a different outlook on my life, my education and my future. At last I have learnt to understand that nothing one does is going to change circumstances out of their control, not even through anorexia.

A person with *bulimia nervosa* is generally of average weight or slightly overweight and experiences a repeated compulsion to eat large amounts of usually high-kilojoule food. This is followed by purging to relieve guilt and get rid of the kilojoules. The cycle is repeated, and the scale of the binges increases.

The condition is most prevalent among women in their late teens and early twenties, often in association with depression and other mood disorders.

Dramatic fluctuations in weight are very common. Vomiting and laxative use may initially cause weight loss, but because they seldom rid the body of all the food that was eaten—and because of the body's natural resistance to sudden changes in weight—the sufferer usually regains the weight and more.

If you suspect your child might have bulimia or anorexia, let her know you are concerned and there to help, and consult a doctor or community health centre for more information and advice.

Psychosis

The term psychosis is used to indicate a serious mental illness which causes the sufferer to lose contact with reality and behave and think in a bizarre, odd or extreme way. The signs of this may be confused thinking, delusions, hallucinations, changed feelings, mood swings and changed behaviour. The usual age of onset is in the teenage or young adult period. The teenager has a lack of insight that there is anything wrong so it is important that people around them ensure they get the right help. Psychosis should be treated as a medical emergency because early treatment results in much better outcomes. Late treatment may sentence a young person to lifelong disability.

Psychoses are biological disorders of the brain and sometimes these conditions require lifelong management. While the specific causes are not yet known, genetic predisposition, abnormal brain functioning and environmental factors contribute. The onset of a psychotic illness and lack of response to treatment are sometimes related to the use of illegal drugs including cannabis. There are different types of psychosis, the main forms being Bipolar Disorder and Schizophrenia.

Bipolar disorder

In adults, bipolar disorder is sometimes referred to as *manic depressive psychosis*. Bipolar disorder often starts during adolescence, but it may not be spotted or correctly diagnosed because there's not yet a pattern of recurrent episodes.

Bipolar disorder is characterised by extreme and often rapid mood swings, from intense sadness to elation, prolonged elevated mood, increased energy, irritability, 'speeded-up' thinking and speech and reduced need to sleep. Parents of young sufferers often say it feels as if they're dealing with a different person, someone they no longer know. The teenager may have days when he is depressed, irritable and negative and withdraws from family and friends. Suddenly he may change back to his usual self or switch, perhaps for shorter periods, to being over-active, giggly, over-talkative, silly and impulsive. In conversation, he may skip from one topic to another and may not listen to the responses of others.

He may become uncharacteristically rude or aggressive or promiscuous and take risks with sex, drugs, or dangerous activities such as driving without a licence. These over-energetic, even frantic behaviours are termed *hypomania*. The switches between depressed and hypomanic behaviour may be fast, occurring even within the space of a day, or come in longer waves with episodes months apart.

Bipolar disorder tends to be chronic and recurrent, but early diagnosis and treatment including medication and psychological and family support are the best ways to help a young person understand her condition and form a 'working partnership' with her therapist. Some people with bipolar disorder may need to spend time in hospital.

Schizophrenia

Schizophrenia is a form of psychosis that often starts with depression, anxiety and extreme fearfulness. Contrary to the popular stereotype, schizophrenia has nothing to do with split personality, but it is a serious disorder that affects one in 100 Australians at some time in their lives and may become a lifelong disorder. It most often begins in early adult life, but can occur earlier. It is three times as common in young men, but by the late twenties equal numbers of men and women are affected.

A person with schizophrenia has hallucinations, hears voices, sees things that aren't there, or tastes, feels, or smells things that are not real. She might also develop delusional ideas, believing her actions or others' are controlled by outside forces such as aliens, celebrities, computers, or radio waves. The person might also think and talk in a confusing and chaotic way. A person with schizophrenia also usually loses motivation and energy and withdraws from social contact. Sometimes she or he has symptoms of both schizophrenia and severe depression; this condition is referred to as a *schizoaffective disorder.*

Schizophrenia in adolescents may be heralded by increasing emotional and behavioural problems and a sense that their thinking and perceptions are changing in ways they can't control. Early detection and treatment with antipsychotic medications of pre-onset psychotic symptoms improve the long-term outcome, and may even help prevent or limit some of the gradual changes in brain function that are associated with chronic schizophrenia.

Early schizophrenia is usually treated with lower doses and shorter courses of antipsychotic medication, which results in fewer side effects and better compliance with medication. As the illness is usually associated with loss of insight, a teenager may not readily seek help. Involuntary inpatient treatment is required if the young person is at risk of harming themselves or others. The symptoms can be very frightening for the person affected and the people around them. Support, education, reassurance and assertive clinical management are required to prevent lifelong disability.

The use of cannabis is increasingly associated with the onset or recurrence of symptoms of schizophrenia. In vulnerable young people, cocaine, amphetamines and other stimulant substances also contribute to an increased risk of suffering from a psychosis. Sometimes the use of these substances is prompted by the young person trying to escape from their perplexing symptoms. Unfortunately, this attempt at self-medication might further act to increase the risk of psychosis. Therefore, the treatment of young people with a psychosis often includes helping them to avoid the use of substances such as cannabis, tobacco (nicotine), alcohol and stimulants.

Two troubled teenagers
Tranh

Tranh was sixteen when he started refusing to eat with his family. He'd retreat to his bedroom, often locking the door, muttering incoherent comments. He was a gifted student, but began to focus obsessively on trying to solve self-posed mathematical questions that his teacher could not understand or writing long, incomplete essays about racism. At times he would cry uncontrollably for hours but be unable to tell his parents what was wrong. Some nights, he would wander away from home. His father would usually find him pacing up and down at the Catholic church the family attended. Tranh's parents were angry, thinking he was wasting his intelligence and educational opportunities. A friend told them that a year or so earlier Tranh had regularly smoked marijuana at sleep-over parties; the parents had thought that the boys were just playing computer games and table tennis. The friend said that on the nights when Tranh wandered away from home, he usually smoked marijuana before wandering to the church.

Tranh was in the early phases of a psychotic illness which developed into schizophrenia. He dropped out of school and was not diagnosed until six months later, after he started shouting incoherently at the back of the church during a service and the priest called the police. His parents had not known what to do.

They initially saw their son's problems as mere teenage waywardness, and didn't think their GP would be able to help.

Tranh needed prolonged treatment, initially in hospital then in a community unit. He has now returned to his studies and lives independently in supported accommodation and his symptoms are well controlled with antipsychotic medication.

Ben

Ben lived in a river town in the country. His family had a close, loving relationship. His parents were keen participants in community sports and the local music group. His two older siblings had graduated from school and were now working. Fifteen-year-old Ben had always been shy and sensitive. Rough games would make him cry and complain that the other children were being unfair. Ben had always had a small group of close friends who played quietly, built models or read.

It happened so slowly that his parents didn't really notice it, but in hindsight they agreed that for about the last year, Ben had been going out less, not always finishing his homework and becoming increasingly intolerant of his older brother's and sister's lifestyle, which he saw as selfish. He'd also had bursts of silliness, getting up early and cooking elaborate breakfasts out of the blue, or detouring to the shops on his way home from school to buy tins of oysters. Things came to a head when a caring teacher confidentially showed the parents an essay Ben had written about a character called 'Black Death' who saw no point in life and was working to kill off young people who were selfish. Ben also talked about methods of drowning.

Ben's parents took him to a doctor, and he was eventually diagnosed with bipolar disorder. It turned out that his grandmother had probably had depression and a great-uncle had committed suicide. Ben and his parents now understand that he has an illness that runs in the family and requires permanent medication, just like a person with diabetes needs insulin.

The messages to remember

- Depression can sometimes be an early-warning sign of other mental health problems. Always take depression seriously and seek help. Don't wait.

- Psychosis should be treated with antipsychotic medication as a medical emergency, to ensure a good outcome.

- Indicators of potential mental illness—a deterioration in school performance, uncharacteristic irritability or anger, withdrawal and suspiciousness, changes in eating habits and sleep patterns—may appear gradually and thus be missed at first.

- There is a strong relationship between mental illness and high-risk behaviour, including promiscuous and unsafe sexual activity.

- Spotting and treating mental illness early can prevent more serious problems from developing.

- In most cases, your local GP, Community Health Centre or Mental Health Service can give advice about getting the right help.

Part 4

Young people in crisis: how can we help?

The first concern, always and for everybody involved, must be safety.

The most mature decision I have ever made was to seek help. This was at a time when I felt completely hopeless.

—Kim, aged sixteen

Teenagers in crisis will often react angrily or aggressively against parents and teachers. The challenge for those on the receiving end is, first, to weather the storm. The next step is to find a positive way out of the crisis while continuing to provide support. The first concern, always and for everybody involved, must be safety. Sometimes that means enlisting professional help.

When home becomes a battleground and the situation has become entrenched or seems to be deteriorating, more drastic measures may be called for. Young people who are violent must be warned that the police may be called. When things get this extreme, it can be necessary to arrange for an angry or out-of-control teenager to stay with an adult relative or friend while things cool off.

It can be difficult to keep communication lines open in times of crisis. Sometimes it is more important to know what questions to ask than to think we have all the answers. Sometimes it is better to listen than to advise or intervene.

In Part 4 we look at the challenges of:

1. Acting out and risk-taking
2. Suicidal behaviour and self-harm
3. Alcohol and other drug use

14
Acting out: a cry for help

The deeper that sorrow carves into your being, the
more joy you can contain.
—Kahlil Gibran

A cting out occurs when a young person, often in the throes of inner conflict or distress, does something eccentric, violent or impulsive to avoid experiencing painful feelings. For example, a teenager may be unhappy because his parents have separated, but instead of talking about this feeling to others (let alone to himself), he may go out drinking or stay out all night, revelling in danger and tempting fate.

The teenager may briefly feel better (or less sad) even without understanding quite why he's doing these things. But the bad feelings inevitably come back with a vengeance. Meanwhile, the underlying feelings remain hidden and unfaced. For this reason acting out must be viewed as a cry for help.

Dealing with risky behaviours

Acting out may involve risk-taking. When this is associated with depression, it may start posing a threat to life. It is normal for parents to worry about risk-taking, but preferable for them not to panic.

Young people are by nature experimental. How else can they work out what is not safe and what is sensible and right for them? Only the most timid and fearful of parents would want their teenager never to take chances. That would mean they never grew up.

Obviously, however, there's more to deliberate risk-taking than mere experimentation. As we saw in Chapter 1, the adolescent brain is still developing, and the highest-level areas, responsible for social judgement and self-control, may not be completely mature until we hit our twenties. While teenage brains may be constructed in a way that makes their owners more open to ideas and more amenable to change, this also makes them more likely to take risks.

For teenagers in emotional distress, taking risks may offer a way to avoid feelings and conflicts that are too painful to face. It may give a sense of exhilaration that temporarily erases feelings of inadequacy, and worthlessness. Or it may reflect suicidal wishes. Sometimes, risk-taking is associated with a lack of satisfaction; if you're in rotten circumstances (homeless and unemployed, for example), perhaps getting high is the best thing going.

Parents may inadvertently worsen teenage risk-taking in a number of ways:

- By the behaviour they 'model'—for example, a teenager is twice as likely to smoke if both parents smoke.
- By the behaviour they disapprove of, especially when the disapproval is expressed in a stern 'It's bad for you and you must not do it' tone. This gives kids something to rebel against.
- By the behaviour they 'set up' through subtle messages. Calling a child 'My big, strong son, the tough athlete' might lead him to believe he is bigger, stronger and tougher than he actually is.

- By behaviour they avoid—for example, not eating well, not exercising and not setting appropriate limits. If we say, 'It's your life, do what you want!' our child might take us at our word.

There are influences in the outside world that are beyond our control as parents. Naturally, young people would be a lot safer if powerful motorbikes, hotted-up cars, firearms, drugs and the internet did not exist. But they do, and there's not much we can do about it.

On the one hand, there are the depressing realities of troubled and confused families, unemployment and uncertainty about the future, giving rise to an understandable 'what the hell' attitude. On the other hand, the mass media delivers a constant bombardment of sexual innuendoes, violence, so-called glamour and glitz, and alcohol and tobacco advertising, a package thoroughly deserving of the label 'ill-health promotion'! Add to all these the absence of a recognised social status for the young, and we have a recipe for trouble. Statistical evidence indicates that risky behaviours are interconnected. There are definite correlations, for example, between the use of alcohol and the use of other drugs such as tobacco and marijuana. The greater the use of drugs, the more likely the involvement in other risky behaviours such as unsafe sex, aggression and delinquency.

What can be done to prevent dangerous risk-taking?

We accept that our kids are going to take risks now and then. What we don't want is for them to get out of their depth, with potentially dire consequences.

To protect kids we have to start early, encouraging them to understand and care for their bodies. Whether they'll do so has a lot to do with how we look after our own! If we are into the medicine cabinet at the slightest twinge or heavy smokers or drinkers, our teenagers will copy us, nothing surer.

It is important to set limits. We need to negotiate with kids about the time they should be home, discuss with them how to drive safely and resist the temptation to drink too much, and of course tell them never to drink and drive or get into a car with a driver who's been drinking (see the pledges of safety in Chapter 5). But when we discuss non-negotiable limits, we should also take the time to listen to our teenagers—lecturing them, as tempting as it can be, rarely has the desired effect. Providing reasons why you have set a non-negotiable limit is preferable to saying: 'Just because I said so', 'don't ask questions', and 'just do what I tell you to'.

Beyond this, all forms of stress management are also relevant here—encouraging optimism and assertiveness will help our child to calculate risk. There is no special formula for preventing drug use among teenagers, or any other form of risk-taking, for that matter. Kids get together and do what they're going to do, no matter what. Whatever it is, some will do it, some won't. Precious little of what young people do can be controlled by any heroic acts of parental will. In fact, once we've had our quiet and sensible say, established trust and maintained open communication, set the best example we can and prayed hard, the rest is really up to them.

Homelessness

We don't know exactly how many Australian teenagers are living on the streets or moving from one short-term home to the next. Every night in Australia, 105 000 people are homeless, including 20 000 12–18 year-olds and over 12 000 children under 12. It's thought that up to 60 per cent of homeless children leave home because they've been physically or sexually abused or because the tension and conflict at home are intolerable.

When a teenager runs away from home it is usually an act of desperation. Young runaways (or throwaways as the case may be) typically have rock bottom self-esteem. Many feel they have no history worth remembering and no future, only emptiness. Not only do they believe nobody gives a damn about them but they feel, and usually are, powerless to change their circumstances. They also grieve the loss of their families, who may be out of sight, but are never out of mind for long.

In their often desperate struggle for survival, drugs, prostitution, violence and brutality become part of homeless kids' world. High-risk lifestyles make them vulnerable to sexually transmitted diseases including hepatitis and HIV/AIDS.

Teenage boys and girls in this situation need access to strong and caring adults, which is easier said than done. They tend to avoid hospitals, doctors and social workers and have little trust in 'do gooders' and authority figures.

Of course, not all young people who run away from home are depressed or escaping abuse and neglect. Sometimes there's an element of 'acting out' and the situation may not be sinister or dangerous.

Andy, aged sixteen, had seemed restless and unsettled for some months. Conflict over relatively minor issues had characterised his relationship with his parents who were concerned about his mood and general behaviour. He was underachieving at school, staying out late with friends—even on some week nights—and resisting efforts to engage him in conversation and family-based activities. They suspected he might be 'smoking dope', which was adamantly denied, and were wondering if he might be depressed or troubled about something. Andy had recently become involved with a girl (also 16) who seemed more mature than her years, a topic he was also not willing to discuss with them.

One day, at the beginning of the school holidays, Andy suddenly packed a bag and declared he was 'leaving home'. It took minimal detective work on his mother's part to discover that he had gone initially to a friend's house (subsequently moving in with his girlfriend's family) and was comfortable and safe. They felt they had little recourse but to leave well enough alone and allow the scenario to play out. Upon spontaneously returning home some weeks later, Andy was clearly in better humour. No parental inquisition was undertaken, in fact, little was said about his period of elective absence. Family life resumed its normal warmth and rhythm and he returned to school at the beginning of the new Term.

There is wisdom at times in under-reacting to testing behaviour. In Andy's case, whatever was going on with him at the time, getting some space from his own family seemed to help.

Juvenile crime and violence

There is a strong connection between depression and delinquency, relevant in at least a third of cases. Quite often too, young people getting into difficulty with the law are reacting to environmental influences such as a disrupted or dangerous home life. Homelessness and offending behaviour also often go hand in hand, part of a downhill spiral involving deteriorating health as well as deteriorating behaviour. Meaningful relationships with mature and caring adults are the cornerstones of effective work with troubled adolescents. When things are going badly wrong, an important question for someone to ask is: 'Is this young person depressed?'

It is important to emphasise that the vast majority of people with mental illness are not violent or aggressive. In fact, people with mental illness are more likely to be the victims of violence, bullying and discrimination.

The messages to remember

- Risk-taking behaviour is sometimes a form of 'acting out' and should be interpreted as a cry for help.

- Parents can help by their monitoring and supervision of their teenage children, especially during the early adolescent years, and should negotiate rules of safety.

- Not all teenagers who leave home, even in circumstances of acrimony and family strife, are destined to become homeless or to lead a life of crime. However, the possibility of an underlying depression or other mental health problem should be considered and the help of caring adults outside the family enlisted.

15
Suicidal behaviour and self-harm

Often the test of courage is not to die but to live.
—Conte Vittorio Alfieri (1749–1803)

lthough youth suicide rates are falling in Australia and New Zealand, they remain among the highest in the developed world. Suicide is closely related to depression in this age group. Of course, many more young people attempt suicide than actually succeed. The rate of hospitalisation of young people who have harmed themselves is escalating. Although more girls than boys try to kill themselves, boys succeed more often because they are more likely to use an effective method (such as hanging or shooting themselves). A girl might take an overdose of pills (tranquillisers, for example) or cut her wrists, and then call or tell someone. Tragically, some teenagers who make half-hearted attempts end up losing their lives anyway.

The risk of dying by suicide is higher not only if the young person is male but also if they: have previously attempted or threatened suicide, have a history of depression or suicide in the family, have suffered depression, are a high-achieving perfectionist, have psychotic illness, abuse alcohol and other drugs, engage in antisocial, delinquent behaviour, have an eating disorder, have experienced significant losses such as the death of a parent, have chronic unresolved family problems, lack social supports, have experienced a loss of hope, and have a suicide plan.

While suicide is defined as voluntary, intentional, self-inflicted death, there are two other ways in which adolescent suicides may also occur:

- A death ruled accidental (say, in a car or motorcycle accident) may be a disguised suicide
- Suicide can occur indirectly when young people choose to take drugs or maintain a lifestyle that slowly kills them.

It's important to distinguish self-harm from suicidality. In self-harming behaviour, the teenager doesn't want to kill herself but to get relief from overwhelming emotions, for example by cutting herself. This is mostly a problem with young women, and parents often don't know that it's happening. There are three main groups of young people who self-harm: those with post-traumatic stress disorder, those experiencing chronic trauma and abuse, and those who are emotionally unstable. The truly suicidal young person, on the other hand, wants to go to sleep and never wake up. He wants to be gone. He is seeking escape from an intolerable situation or insoluble problem.

Mentioning suicide will not put the idea into someone's head. If we are in any doubt about a young person in distress, it can help to ask a question like, 'Sometimes people who feel this way have thoughts about hurting themselves. Have you ever thought about this?'

When the answer is yes, further questions might be:

- Have you ever thought that life was not worth living?
- Have you ever wished you were dead?

- Have you ever thought about killing yourself?
- Have you ever tried to kill yourself?
- Do you have a plan?

This subject of suicide is complex and distressing and, not surprisingly, many people would rather not think about it. Sometimes, however, we need to—a life may be at stake. When an adolescent commits suicide her parents' grief is surely only deepened by additional feelings of guilt or anger or total bewilderment, by the pain of the police investigation and coronial inquest and by the social stigma still attached to suicide. In a poignant newspaper article, a mother whose daughter had committed suicide once made this plea: 'If you are a teenager reading this, don't give up on life. Death is a one-way ticket, marked not negotiable. That body in the morgue is no longer yours to make choices with. Suicide is a game where everybody loses—your parents, your friends and, most of all, you.'

More than 90 per cent of depressed and suicidal young people confide in a friend before they take their life. It's extremely important, therefore, to give friends a way to help. Sometimes it's too difficult for one person to deal with the situation. Once a friend is worried, everyone should pull out all the stops. Schools need to encourage students to get together with friends and tell someone in authority. This is a time for dobbing. It is the one situation where it's OK not to keep a secret. The one thing that trumps confidentiality is safety. One seventeen-year-old girl said that when she found out a friend was hurting herself, 'I told my mum and she told my friend's mum. My friend didn't talk to me for ages, but I didn't want to feel the guilt if she had really hurt herself.'

A common trigger for a suicide attempt is a relationship break-up, particularly where the upset person isn't feeling supported.

But there are usually multiple underlying reasons that have been simmering for months or years. Suicide is rarely inexplicable.

If a young person admits to being suicidal, don't brush it off or play it down. Don't be judgemental or get into a panic. Equally, don't promise secrecy, and don't leave the person alone. Take it seriously and get help. If health professionals do not respond to your distress call, be assertive. Make a formal complaint to a senior person, such as the manager of the local mental health service, and try again.

What to do when a teenager threatens suicide

- Talk about it openly. Ask them if they feel so bad that they are thinking of hurting themselves.
- Listen to them. Watch their non-verbal behaviour.
- Tell them that if they need help, you are there for them.
- Offer to go with them to get help.
- Ask them why they want to die.
- Tell them you don't want them to get hurt or die because you will miss them.
- Take time to listen and be with them—time is a precious gift to give.
- Consult a professional if you are concerned about a young person's behaviour.

Appleby, M. and Condonis M. 1990, *Hearing the Cry*, The Rose Foundation, Oakland CA, 1990.

Someone at high risk of suicide requires immediate referral and may have to go to hospital. Here are a few warning signs:

- They have well thought-out plans
- They have a clear idea of where to do it
- The means are readily available
- They have given away most possessions
- They have made arrangements, written a note, made a will
- They have made previous attempts
- They frequently binge or abuse alcohol
- They have marked tunnel vision (think only about death)
- They have marked hostility, even if they deny wanting to die
- They are very disorganised
- They have a negative view of help, or reject help that is offered
- They can't call on help from people close to them
- They have had significant recent losses e.g. parental divorce, death of a close relative, break-up with a boyfriend or girlfriend
- They shrink from getting involved in activities
- They feel or seem helpless, withdrawn, isolated
- They are in either a state of panic and agitation or a state of withdrawn, secretive calmness; they may feel an odd, detached happiness because the decision has been made.
- They have severe depression

Here are some important questions that parents might hear a psychiatrist, GP or counsellor ask their depressed son or daughter who is in crisis:

- **Can you tell me what is happening?**
- **What has happened to upset you?**
- **What is playing on your mind?**

- What needs to change?
- What can I do to help or support you?
- What is the argument in your head?
- What would you be doing if the depression were not there?
- Do my concerns concern you? Why or why not?
- Who are the people you trust, feel close to or have things in common with?
- Can you contact them now and talk to them?
- How do you know that people care?
- What are the questions you would like me to ask?

Together with the teenager, parents and counsellors may negotiate a crisis plan, guided by the answers to these questions:

- What is the behaviour of concern?
- What triggers it?
- What are the dos and don'ts?
- What works and what doesn't?
- Who has what role and what responsibility?
- Do the adults know what to do in an after-hours situation?
- Do the teenager and parents each have a copy of the plan, in case of crisis?

What if a teenager at risk will not seek help? It can be very difficult for parents or teachers when a teenager not only refuses direct help but also refuses to seek help himself. If a young person lives away from the family, it can help just to keep in touch, send supportive cards or letters, or give them written information and educational brochures on mental illness. It may also help to get some leaflets about local youth services or lists of GP names and clinics, make your teenager aware of these services, and reassure them about confidentiality. It is unfortunate that some young people have to reach crisis point before they will accept help, but if they have some useful telephone numbers or websites, they are more likely to seek the right help at this point (see Appendix).

If a young person is at risk of harming themselves or others, they may require involuntary admission and treatment in a psychiatric hospital.

The messages to remember

When young people are in crisis or a danger to themselves:

- Listen, be patient, don't judge

- Seek help from a crisis service—usually the local mental health service or even the police, if necessary

- Stay nearby to keep them safe

- Always take seriously comments about not wanting to live.

16
Alcohol and
other drugs

*What we do to survive is often different from what
we need to do in order to live.*
—Dr Rachel Remen

A young person who is depressed might seek relief in alcohol
or illicit drugs. These drugs are also likely to cause or worsen
a depression.

Most young people know the harm alcohol and illicit drugs
can do. Yet their abuse is common, even among under-eighteens.
According to the Australian National Council on Drugs:

- In a single given week, about one in ten twelve- to
  seventeen-year-olds report binge drinking or drinking at
  harmful levels.
- One in seven secondary school students report using
  cannabis in the previous twelve months.
- One in twenty-five secondary school students
  are estimated to have used amphetamines in the
  previous year.

As we saw in Chapter 7, many adolescents experiment with alcohol and other drugs, but only a small minority go on to become serious substance abusers. Those at greatest risk of dependence and addiction are young people with depression and other mental-health problems who consume alcohol or illicit drugs to escape their anguish. Other predictors of persistent alcohol and drug abuse are: engaging in antisocial behaviour, initiating alcohol and drugs at an early age, repeatedly getting heavily intoxicated, hanging out with older drug-users, being labelled by friends or adults as a substance abuser, losing a parent during the pre-teen or teenage years, and poor family relationships, particularly with parents.

Signs of regular alcohol and drug-taking include:

- A change in school attendance (frequently absent or late) or achievement (sloppy homework, apathy and lack of effort)
- New friends and a reluctance to introduce them to the family
- Dishevelled clothing, unhealthy appearance and total neglect of personal hygiene
- Red eyes, dilated or constricted pupils, drowsiness and confusion
- Marked changes in emotional state, with unusual aggressiveness, temper flare-ups, excessive tiredness or social withdrawal
- Furtive behaviour, including lying, stealing or borrowing money (because drugs cost money), an unexplained need for more money
- Concerns expressed by friends, their parents or other adults.

When considering the longer term effects of excessive alcohol and other drug consumption on the body, it can lead to serious and persistent changes such as brain shrinkage, particularly in young brains, even after withdrawal.

If a teenager admits to abusing alcohol or other drugs, here are some sensible steps to follow: do some reading and become better informed about the subject (see Appendix), clarify the facts, clarify your own concerns so you can approach your teenager as a concerned and rational adult, try not to moralise. Detailed information about drugs is only a phone call away, and there are many sources of advice and help (see Appendix).

Signs of addiction
- Spending a great deal of time using or trying to buy the substance
- Using it more often than one intends
- Thinking about reducing use
- Making repeated unsuccessful efforts to reduce use
- Giving up important social, family or occupational activities to use it
- Developing a craving for the substance including drinking alcohol earlier in the day
- Reporting agitation and withdrawal symptoms after stopping using it, for example waking with a hangover after a drinking session.

Withdrawal symptoms

If a person who is dependent on alcohol or another drug suddenly stops taking it, they will experience withdrawal symptoms, because their body has to readjust to functioning without the drug. These may include: cravings, disorientation and poor concentration, tremors, decreased energy, extreme fatigue and exhaustion, apathy and limited ability to experience pleasure, irritability, depression, anxiety, panic, paranoia, headaches or general aches and pains, hunger and increased appetite, disturbed and restless sleep.

Here are some suggestions to make if your teenager is having withdrawal symptoms:

- Understand what alcohol and drug abuse is doing to your body;
- Identify people who will support you;
- Avoid triggers which encourage you to use, such as socialising with people who use;
- Practise self-talk saying, 'No, thanks, I don't do that any more';
- Beat cravings with relaxing activities or exercise;
- Start a diary and record your feelings and level of craving. Cravings will continue if you continue to feed the habit;
- Reassure yourself that the withdrawal symptoms will pass and try to ride through them. Withdrawal symptoms usually last four days to two weeks;
- Reward yourself with things other than drugs and alcohol;
- If you relapse and find yourself using again, don't give up. Ask yourself what you will do differently next time. What do you like about the drug? What would be good about reducing its use? What made it hard to cut down?

Treatment options

When children are binge drinking or abusing other drugs, families need outside support. Unfortunately, there are relatively few alcohol and other drug treatment options available in Australia. Your GP, community health centre, or drug and alcohol service can offer behavioural therapy. Some programs aim for a drug-free lifestyle; others regard abstinence as only one of a number of strategies to reduce the harm from the person's drug use.

Some treatment options include: outpatient or inpatient counselling, group therapy, detoxification and medication. Treatment is more effective if it's tailored to suit a young person's circumstances, and usually involves a combination of methods. Effective treatment addresses underlying problems such as depression, promotes personal development, and helps the young person re-engage with their family, friends and the wider community.

In case of collapse

If a young person collapses after abusing alcohol or other drugs, it is a medical emergency. A quick response, along the following lines can save their life:

- Assess their level of consciousness.
- Immediately remove any obstruction to their breathing.
- Begin mouth-to-mouth resuscitation if the breathing has stopped.
- Feel the pulse. If there is no pulse begin cardiopulmonary resuscitation (CPR).
- If the person is unconscious but still breathing, roll them on their side and into the 'recovery position'. Gently tilt her head back so her tongue does not block her airway. Do not leave her on her back in case she chokes on her vomit.
- Call an ambulance urgently. Dial 000 without delay. Stay with the person until the ambulance arrives. Provide the ambulance officers with as much information as you can about what drugs were taken,

how long ago, and any pre-existing medical conditions.
Ambulance officers are not obliged to involve the police.

Illicit drugs

Cannabis

What does it look like? There are three main forms: marijuana
(dried leaves and flowers), hashish (dried resin in blocks), and
hash oil (thick oily liquid rarely found in Australia).

How is it taken? Smoked, cooked.

Street names: Grass, pot, hash, weed, reefer, dope, herb, mull,
Buddha, ganja, joint, stick, buckets, cones, smoko, head.

Every year, more people, mostly teenagers, become regular cannabis
users. Parents worry that smoking dope puts teenagers on a downhill
run to heroin. This is by no means inevitable, because most use it
only as a recreational drug. But smokers are likely to come in contact
with people who peddle a variety of drugs, and this is a worry.

Heated debates about the ill-effects of dope and whether or not
laws should be changed rage on. Some young people believe that
cannabis is in some way safer than cigarettes or alcohol. This is
false. Cannabis is a depressant drug that slows down the central
nervous system, delaying messages between the brain and the body.
The short-term effects (which last for two to four hours) include:

- Increased awareness of sensation and colour, laughter
  and a sense of well-being, an altered perception of time
  and space;
- Stimulation of appetite;
- A dry mouth, dizziness, bloodshot eyes and, in some
  users, panic attacks and feelings of paranoia;
- Impaired coordination; problems with memory and the
  ability to think logically, confusion and hallucinations.

The long-term effects of cannabis are extremely worrying:

- Dependence can develop, and there is a characteristic withdrawal syndrome. Chronic marijuana users also become very psychologically dependent and cannot or will not believe that their habit is causing them harm.
- Habituated users lose energy, drive, short-term memory and concentration. These effects persist long after people stop using the drug and may not be reversible, suggesting physiological changes in the brain.
- Heavy use can impair the lungs. Cannabis is often mixed with loose tobacco to help it burn better. This has far more tar than commercial cigarettes, increasing users' risk of lung cancer and chronic bronchitis as well as cancer of the mouth, tongue and jaw.
- The active chemical in cannabis (tetrahydro-cannabinol) can precipitate a wide variety of acute, disabling psychiatric syndromes, notably acute anxiety or panic and brief psychosis. Paranoia is particularly troubling to heavy cannabis users and symptoms can persist for up to a year after they stop using the drug.

Cannabis users have higher than average rates of depression and anxiety. Psychiatrists recognise that one reason for high rates of youth suicide and adolescent depression is the heavy use of dope. The receptor sites in the brain on which cannabis works are the same ones that antidepressant medication acts on. Cannabis competes with antidepressant medication, blocking it from these sites and preventing it from working. Cannabis may produce transient relief from symptoms of depression, but rebound depression follows in a couple of hours. It can be difficult to convince depressed teenagers to stop taking marijuana because they briefly feel better when they are on it.

Inhalants

About one in three high school students admits to having tried sniffing solvents or aerosols like glue, petrol, lighter fluid, cleaning fluid and paint thinner. Sniffing is done by girls and boys in about equal numbers and peaks at about thirteen to fourteen. After that, most sniffers give it up.

Street names: Glue, gas, sniff, huff, chroming, as in the use of chrome paint, poppers.

The effects of sniffing include sensations of happiness, euphoria and relaxation, which last from one to three hours. The high is similar to that of extreme drunkenness. Adverse effects include drowsiness, agitation, flu-like symptoms such as sneezing, coughing and runny nose, disorientation, problems with coordination, nausea and vomiting, diarrhoea, unpleasant breath, nose bleeds and sores, and reckless behaviour.

Adolescents seem largely unaware of the danger of sniffing, but sudden death by cardiac arrest can occur, even on the first try. Depending on the solvent used, chronic sniffing may damage the nervous system, kidneys, liver or heart. Such chronic abuse is rare, usually occurring only in deeply troubled young people.

Heroin

What does it look like? Heroin comes as white to pink or brown granules or rocks packaged in foils (aluminium foil) or small balloons.

How is it taken? It's most commonly injected into a vein but can be snorted or heated and the vapour inhaled referred to as 'chasing the dragon'.

Street names: Smack, skag, dope, H, junk, hammer, slow, gear, harry, horse, rock.

This highly addictive narcotic drug gives sensations of euphoria and contentment. The adverse effects include nausea and a slowing down of bodily functions including breathing, blood pressure and digestion, causing drowsiness and constipation. The pupils of the eyes become smaller. In an overdose, breathing becomes very slow, body temperature drops and heartbeat becomes irregular. This can quickly lead to death. Combining heroin with other depressant drugs greatly increases its effects, and a relatively light dose of heroin can thus turn into a heavy dose.

Street heroin is usually a mixture of pure heroin and other substances such as talcum powder, baking powder, starch, glucose or quinine. Sometimes other drugs, such as amphetamines and barbiturates, are also added. Sharing needles and syringes increases the risk of contracting hepatitis or HIV. Dependence can be psychological or physical. Withdrawal symptoms may include insomnia, restlessness, diarrhoea, stomach cramps and vomiting, and may resemble a bout of the flu.

Although only about two in 100 Australians over fourteen have used heroin, deaths from heroin are increasing and the social cost in terms of crime and the drain on the health system is significant.

LSD (lysergic acid diethylamide)

What does it look like? Pure LSD is a white odourless powder. It usually comes in the form of liquid, tablets or capsules, or squares of gel and is often diluted with another substance, such as sugar, or soaked onto sheets of blotting paper.

How is it taken? It can be swallowed, sniffed, injected or smoked.

Street names: Acid, trips, tabs, T.

This drug heightens perception and causes hallucinations. The pupils enlarge, the heart may speed up. There may be nausea and loss of appetite, chills and flushing, shaking, paranoia, confusion and acute panic. Long-term effects can include flashbacks (intense nightmares) which occur days, weeks or even years after last using the drug. People can also become psychologically or physically dependent. LSD can trigger or worsen mental illness.

Amphetamines

What do they look like? Amphetamines can be in the form of powder, tablets, capsules, crystals or red liquid. The tablets or capsules vary in colour, and can be a cocktail of drugs, binding agents, caffeine and sugar.

How are they taken? Most commonly, they are swallowed, injected (in the case of methamphetamine) or smoked. They are also snorted or sniffed.

Street names: Speed, up, fast, louee, goey, whiz, pep pills, uppers.

Amphetamines stimulate the central nervous system, providing a rush of energy and confidence and reducing fatigue. They speed everything up, including the heartbeat and breathing. The pupils may get bigger and the mouth dry, and the user may start to sweat. Amphetamines also cause impulsiveness, irritability and loss of appetite. High doses can cause headaches, dizziness, blurred vision, tremors, irregular heartbeat, stomach cramps and loss of coordination. Due to the unknown strength and mix of street amphetamines, some single-dose users have collapsed after overdosing and others have had strokes, heart failure and seizures.

Ice refers to crystal methamphetamine, which is more potent than other forms of the drug. As well as a more extreme high, it has stronger side effects and a worse 'comedown'. Paranoia, hallucinations, irritability, depression, hostility and aggression are particularly common and unpleasant side effects of ice.

Amphetamines have an important therapeutic role, however. If properly prescribed and used, they can safely and effectively treat attention deficit hyperactivity disorder (ADHD) but even in these situations might have to be discontinued for adverse side effects such as anxiety, depression and irritability.

Ecstasy

What does it look like? Ecstasy usually comes in the form of small white or yellow or brownish tablets of various sizes, shapes and designs.

How is it taken? The 'tabs' are swallowed or crushed and snorted. They can be inserted into the anus from where the drug is absorbed—this is referred to as 'shafting' or 'shelving'. Injecting ecstasy has recently become more popular.

Street names: Ecstasy is a street term for a range of drugs that are similar in structure to MDMA (methylenedioxymethamphetamine). Ecstasy is also known as E, Vitamin E, XTC, eccy and the love drug.

Ecstasy is like both amphetamines and LSD in chemical structure and effect. It is a popular party drug because it gives users a sense of closeness and intimacy, and feelings of love and affection. It also causes hallucinations, stimulates thirst and can overheat the body. Death may occur if ecstasy is taken after excessive drinking, as in the well-known case of Anna Wood. New research suggests the drug causes permanent brain damage—it can impair memory, even when taken infrequently, and puts users at risk of developing a Parkinson's-like condition and other disorders.

Fantasy

What does it look like? Gamma-hydroxybutyrate (GHB), or fantasy, is a colourless, odourless, bitter or salty-tasting liquid usually sold in small bottles or vials. It also comes as a crystal powder.

How is it taken? It's mostly taken orally, but occasionally people inject it.

Street names: Fantasy, grievous bodily harm (GBH), liquid ecstasy and liquid E.

Fantasy is another party drug that has depressant effects.

Cocaine

What does it look like? Cocaine hydrochloride is a white, odourless powder. Cocaine may be mixed, or 'cut', with other substances such as sugar, baking soda and talcum powder. Crack is a very pure form of cocaine sold in the form of small crystals or rocks.

How is it taken? Cocaine may be snorted or injected. Crack is smoked in pipes or mixed with tobacco or marijuana in cigarettes.

Street names: C, vitamin C, coke, flake, nose candy, snow, dust, white, white lady, toot, crack, rock, freebase.

Cocaine causes exhilaration and a heightened sense of awareness and alertness, and reduces fatigue and sensations of pain. The adverse effects include anxiety, paranoia and possible addiction. Users may have enlarged pupils and a fast heartbeat and feel sexually aroused. Large doses can cause extreme aggression and hallucinations. As with other stimulant drugs, overdose can cause death from seizures, heart attacks, brain haemorrhage, kidney failure and stroke.

What do young people say about drug use?

I know a few people who are caught up in the drug scene but I don't know what to say to them. I have a few friends who smoke mull. They say: 'We're more relaxed—life's easier.' A guy I know uses speed. He says he can get up and dance all night and drugs are cheaper than alcohol. But these kids usually end up hurting their friends with their lies.

People say drugs are OK—I am just having fun. They are denying that they're really hurting themselves. You can't tell people to stop using drugs unless you offer them something else to do. Sometimes you can't do anything until the person wants to stop themselves. It's easier to forget about your problems than to deal with them.

Some people who try to stop smoking dope can't, because their friends all smoke and it's too hard. It's easier to say yes than no. Quick fixes seem more tolerable than long-term solutions.

Young people are drawn to drugs so strongly because, unfortunately, it seems to us that there is no other way to enjoy life. There is simply no hope in today's society. Take the government, for instance. They are constantly pushing the statistics onto us. 'Half the youth are drug addicts, half of them are unemployed, and the rest of the world is lost in murder, rape, war and money.' Hearing that every day is going to give us hope for our future? I doubt it.

The problem is that drug use is a cool thing to do. They should activate a non-phony campaign on young people's level that makes smoking and drugs seem daggy.

What drugs and alcohol do is give us a false sense of hope, confidence and peace, and we use them because we find it hard to believe that things can be achieved without them. But once you have built up a true sense of hope and confidence there is absolutely no need for drugs. I think society realises that drugs are a major problem. At most schools, drugs are a taboo subject.

You get told that drugs are bad in a million different ways, but no one has the guts to give us the real hard facts. It is no wonder that young people use drugs when they are all around us but we are only given tidbits of information. We are young, we are learning, we are trying to find out the facts of life and it is really sad that we are given the impression that the only way to find out about them is to use them. There needs to be a compulsory program at every school that clearly shows the devastating effects of drug use. Guest speakers—(real young people, not just celebrities like Angry Anderson!) who use, have overcome their use, or who have ended up with hepatitis C or AIDS and are very likely to die, need to be brought right in close to us, to scare the shit out of us.

If you think your teenager is using illicit drugs, consult your GP or the drug and alcohol worker at your local community health service. All these drugs are dangerous, and regular use and abuse is a sign something is seriously wrong.

The messages to remember

- Alcohol and drug abuse are very often associated with mental health problems. Sometimes people use these substances because they have depression or another mental illness. Far from helping, though, drugs can worsen the problem. Sometimes they cause mental illness.

- Scare tactics and zero tolerance seem like good ideas, but these approaches are rarely effective. Many young people will experiment with alcohol and drugs even if they know they're dangerous. A supportive, harm-reduction approach is best. Parents should try to inform their teenagers of the risks, discuss the issue openly and try to understand the underlying problems.

Part 5
Where to from here?

Youth depression is a serious problem.

Youth depression is a serious problem. It can rob young people of their future and potential, wreck lives and even end them. It upsets relationships, interferes with school and learning, messes up family life and places enormous strain on parents. The burden it places on families and society is as great as that imposed by heart disease and other chronic illnesses.

The good news about youth depression

Yet as we have seen, there is a lot of good news about depression. Young people, parents and Australians generally know a lot more about mental health and depression than they used to. They are no longer as ashamed to talk about depression as they once were. The youth suicide rate is falling, and there are coordinated national efforts to detect and more effectively treat depressed young people.

Throughout history, mental illness has carried a stigma in most societies. Mental illness has variously been viewed as a sign of weakness, a punishment for some failure or sin, and as something one should have the strength of character to just 'snap out of'. But as we've seen, depression is, in reality, an illness of the brain, similar to other illnesses of the body such as diabetes or asthma. Removing the stigma from depression and other mental illnesses encourages people to seek treatment, involves the family and community in caring for sufferers, and promotes recovery.

Over the past decade, with the help of organisations like *beyondblue*, Australians have begun talking openly about depression, accepting it as an illness and understanding how it can be treated. Leaders in politics, sports and entertainment have gone public with their own experiences of depression. Seeing some of their heroes openly acknowledge being depressed has encouraged depressed teenagers to accept treatment and not feel ashamed.

Falling suicide rates

There are several likely reasons for the fall in youth suicide rates. They include government funding of community mental health services, education in schools about mental illness, and better training of GPs and school counsellors in the detection and treatment of depression. Psychological treatments such as cognitive behaviour therapy have also become more available and affordable thanks to Medicare.

Gun owners are obliged by law to store firearms in locked safes and keep ammunition separate from guns. The use of blister packs for medication makes it more difficult for a

depressed teenager to grab a handful of tablets, allowing time
for the impulse to pass.

The fall in the suicide rate has also coincided with wider
availability and prescription of SSRI antidepressants, and may
be partly a result of them.

Finally, the news media have adopted a code of ethics for
reporting about people with mental illness and about acts of
suicide. Mostly they do not report the details of how a suicide
occurred. They often provide help-line and emergency-service
contact numbers at the end of articles or programs on
depression and suicide.

Who's been helping?

Also playing an important role is the sustained hard work of
organisations that promote mental health. LifeLine, the
Samaritans, Kids Help Line and other emergency-call groups all
help to defuse crises and direct depressed young people to
where they can get further support and treatment. Mental Health
promotion organisations such as the Mental Health Foundation
of Australia (*www.mentalhealthvic.org.au*) and *beyondblue: the
national depression initiative* (*www.beyondblue.org.au*), and the
Black Dog Institute in New South Wales, play a powerful role in
educating the public, reducing stigma and training doctors,
health professionals, teachers and youth workers.

Australian research into the nature, causes and treatment of
depression is among the best in the world. Australia has a
number of world-class experts in depression, such as Professor
Gordon Parker of the Black Dog Institute, Professor Ian Hickie of
the University of Sydney's Brain & Mind Research Institute,
Professor Graham Martin, of the University of Queensland,
Professor Patrick McGorry, of Orygen Youth Health in
Melbourne, Professor Sue Spence, of Griffith University, and

Professor Mark Dadds, of the University of New South Wales. Their work has been well supported by many politicians, notably former Victorian Premier Jeff Kennett, who was instrumental in the development of *beyondblue*.

Around Australia there is a growing number of programs, often supported by volunteers and community donations, which help teenagers develop resilience and self-worth. They include the Reach youth program, run by former AFL footballer Jim Stynes, a Koori kids Wilderness project in Gippsland, and Father Chris Riley's Youth Off the Streets in Sydney. Well-planned school camps, sporting clubs with youth skill-development programs and other special-interest groups or clubs that offer positive, rewarding activities also play a vital part in building the emotional resilience of Australian youth.

Headspace, the National Youth Mental Health Foundation, was launched in 2007 to improve mental-health services, improve the skills of doctors and health professionals in the treatment of mental illness, and promote mental health in young people generally. Headspace (*www.headspace.org.au*) is establishing youth-friendly mental-health clinics around Australia.

Primary schools are also looking to implement strategies to support student mental health. KidsMatter is the first national mental health promotion, prevention and early intervention initiative specifically developed for primary schools. With KidsMatter, the school community addresses four key areas critical to student mental health and well-being. These are:

(1) *Positive School Community*: by initiating strategies that develop a sense of belonging and connectedness amongst whole school community as well as enabling staff, students, families and communities to work together to support children's well-being;

(2) *Social and Emotional Learning for Students*: by systematically teaching social and emotional skills to all students;

(3) *Parenting Support and Education*: by providing parents with information about child development and effective parenting strategies as well as facilitating access to services that provide parenting support; and

(4) *Early Intervention for Students Experiencing Mental Health Difficulties*: with teachers and parents being aware of the kinds of mental health difficulties that affect children and the types of support available. A range of information resources have been developed for school staff and parents to support KidsMatter. These include information sheets for parents and resource packs providing more detailed information and links to further information and support. All resources can be downloaded at *www.kidsmatter.edu.au*

The internet is also being enlisted to deliver effective education and treatment programs for anxiety, depression and other mental health problems, with a focus on young people. These are especially helpful for those who are isolated or who live in remote areas. Inspire Foundation, a non-profit organisation that aims to create opportunities for young people to change their world, offers two online services. Reach Out! (*www.reachout.com.au*) provides young people over sixteen with information, support and resources to help them understand mental-health issues, develop resilience, increase coping skills and seek further help when they need it. Its website has had over 7.5 million visits since 1998. An interactive game, Reach Out Central (*www.reachoutcentral.com.au*), helps young people absorb the Reach Out! messages in an enjoyable way. With over two million visits since 1996, ActNow (*www.actnow.com.au*) increases social connectedness and civic engagement by providing young people over sixteen with opportunities to connect with their community by taking action on the issues that they care about.

Effective online help for depression, such as MoodGYM (*www.moodgym.anu.edu.au*), and for anxiety and panic disorder (*www.med.monash.edu.au/mpm-cms/mentalhealth*) is now freely available for those over eighteen.

We end, then, on a note of hope. As fourteen-year-old Thoula said to her therapist at the end of her successful treatment for depression: 'Mum talked to the doctor. Result: even though I couldn't see the point, I came to see you. And now I've got my life back.'

Appendix: Helpful resources

Checklists for mental illnesses taken (with permission) from the *beyondblue* website: *www.beyondblue.org.au*

1. Depression

Have you, for more than two weeks:

- felt sad, down or miserable most of the time?
- lost interest or pleasure in most of your usual activities?

If you answered yes to either of these questions, you may have depression and may like to complete the symptom checklist below. If you did not answer yes to either of these questions, it is unlikely that you have a depressive illness.

Have you:

- lost or gained a lot of weight or
  had a decrease or increase in appetite?
- experienced sleep disturbances?
- felt slowed down, restless or excessively busy?
- felt tired or had no energy?
- felt worthless, excessively guilty or
  felt guilty about things without a good reason?

- had poor concentration or
  had difficulty thinking or
  been very indecisive?
- had recurrent thoughts of death?

Add up the number of ticks for your total score. What does your score mean?
(Assuming you answered 'YES' to question 1 and/or question 2)
4 or less: You are unlikely to be experiencing a depressive illness.
5 or more: It is likely that you may be experiencing a depressive illness.

References
American Psychiatric Association, 1994, *Diagnostic and Statistical Manual of Mental Disorders 4th edn (DSM-IV)*, APA Washington DC, and World Health Organization, 1992–1994, *International classification of diseases and related health problems*, 10th edn, World Health Organization, Geneva.

It is important to note that this checklist provides only a rough guide as to whether you may be experiencing depression. If you're concerned that you or someone you know may have symptoms of depression, it's best to speak to your doctor.

2. Generalised Anxiety Disorder
For **six months** or more, on more days than not, have you:

- felt very worried?
- found it hard to stop worrying?
- found that your anxiety made it difficult for you to do everyday activities (e.g. work, study, see friends and family)?

If you answered yes to **all** of these questions, have you also experienced **three** or more of the following:

- felt restless or on edge
- felt easily tired
- had difficulty concentrating
- felt irritable
- had muscle pain (e.g. sore jaw or back)
- had trouble sleeping (e.g. difficulty falling or staying asleep or restless sleep)?

If you answered yes, it is important to see a doctor.

3. Panic Disorder

Within a 10-minute period, have you felt **four or more** of the following:

- sweaty
- shaky
- increased heart rate
- short of breath
- choked
- nauseous or pain in the stomach
- dizzy, lightheaded or faint
- numb or tingly
- derealisation (feelings of unreality) or depersonalisation (feeling detached from yourself or your surroundings)
- hot or cold flushes
- scared of going crazy
- scared of dying?

If you answered yes to **all** of these questions, have you also:

- felt scared, for one month or more, of experiencing these feelings again?

If you answered yes, it is important to see a doctor.

4. Phobia
Have you felt very nervous when faced with a specific object or situation e.g.:

- flying on an aeroplane
- going near an animal
- receiving an injection
- going to a social event?

Have you avoided a situation that might cause you to face the phobia e.g.:

- needed to change work patterns
- not attending social events
- not getting health check-ups
- found it hard to go about your daily life (e.g. working, studying or seeing friends and family) because you are trying to avoid such situations?

If you answered yes, it is important to see a doctor.

5. Obsessive-compulsive Disorder
Have you:

- had repetitive thoughts or concerns that are not simply about real-life problems (e.g. thoughts that you or people close to you will be harmed)

- done the same activity repeatedly and in a very ordered, precise and similar way each time e.g.:
  - constantly washing your hands or clothes, showering or brushing your teeth
  - constantly cleaning, tidying or rearranging in a particular way things at home, at work or in the car
  - constantly checking that doors and windows are locked and/or appliances are turned off
- felt relieved in the short term by doing these things, but soon felt the need to repeat them
- recognised that these feelings, thoughts and behaviours were unreasonable
- found that these thoughts or behaviours take up more than one hour a day and/or interfered with your normal routine (e.g. working, studying or seeing friends and family)?

If you answered yes, it is important to see a doctor.

6. Post-traumatic Stress Disorder

Have you:

- experienced or seen something that involved death, injury, torture or abuse and felt very scared or helpless
- had upsetting memories or dreams of the event for at least *one* month
- found it hard to go about your daily life (e.g. made it difficult for you to work/study or get along with family and friends)?

If you answered yes to **all** of these questions, have you also experienced at least **three** of the following:

- avoided activities that remind you of the event
- had trouble remembering parts of the event
- felt less interested in doing things you used to enjoy
- had trouble feeling intensely positive emotions (e.g. love or excitement)
- thought less about the future (e.g. about career or family goals)?

and have you experienced at least **two** of the following:

- had difficulties sleeping (e.g. had bad dreams, or found it hard to fall or stay asleep)
- felt easily angry or irritated
- had trouble concentrating
- felt on guard
- been easily startled?

If you answered yes, it is important to see a doctor.

Services and Help/Information Lines
Depression
beyondblue: the national depression initiative
www.beyondblue.org.au
   Fact sheets available in 25 languages; info line: 1300 22 4636
Youthbeyondblue *www.youthbeyondblue.com*
   The youth website of *beyondblue*; focuses on depression,
   anxiety and substance use-related disorders.
SANE Australia *www.sane.org*
   A national charity working for a better life for people affected
   by mental illness; info line: 1800 187 263
Kids Help Line *www.kidshelp.com.au*
   Email and web counselling for children and young people
   aged between five and eighteen; info line: 1800 551 800.
The Mental Health Foundation of Australia
   www.embracethefuture.org.au
   A program to educate young people in strategies and skills
   which promote and sustain resiliency and positive mental
   health
Headspace *www.headspace.org.au*
   Australia's National Youth Mental Health Foundation
Headroom *www.headroom.net.au*
Mensline Australia *www.menslineaus.org.au*
   Relationships, work, fathering, separation, stress;
   info line: 1300 789 978.
Australian Psychological Society *www.psychology.org.au*
   Referral Line: 1800 333 497
Black Dog Institute *www.blackdoginstitute.org.au*
Mood Disorder Association *www.moodsa.info*
Depression and Mood Disorders Association
   www.dmda.mentalhealth.asn.au/supgrp.htm
Mental Health Information Service (NSW) 1800 674 200

Depression and Mood Disorders Association (NSW)
(02) 9816 5688

Panic, Anxiety and Depression Assistance (Vic) (03) 9886 9400

GROW Support Groups (national) *www.grow.net.au*;
info line: 1800 558 268
Information and advice on how to look after the mental
health of young people.

Suicide Prevention

Suicide Helpline *www.suicidehelpline.org.au*

Suicide Prevention Australia *www.suicidepreventionaust.org*

Lifeline *www.lifeline.org.au*; 24-hour helpline: 13 11 14

Anxiety Disorders

Anxiety Recovery Centre Victoria (ARCVic) *www.arcvic.com.au*

Anxiety Disorders Association of Victoria (ADAVIC)
www.adavic.org.au

Reconnexion *www.reconnexion.org.au*
Treating panic, anxiety, depression and tranquilliser
dependency

Social Anxiety Australia *www.socialanxiety.com.au*

Anxiety Disorders Support and Information
www.mentalhealth.asn.au

Anxiety Network Australia *www.anxietynetwork.com.au*

Clinical Research Unit for Anxiety and Depression (CRUfAD)
www.crufad.org

Mental Health Services and Support Groups

Australian Mental Health Consumer Network
www.mmha.org.au

Victorian Mental Illness Awareness Council (VMIAC)
www.vmiac.com.au

Centrelink *www.centrelink.gov.au*
> Information on how people with mental illness and their
> carers can get the support they are entitled to, including
> sickness allowance, disability support pensions and
> psychological treatment.

depressioNet *www.depressionet.com.au*
> depressioNet's forums allow people living with depression to share
> experiences and give and receive support and encouragement.

depression dot com *www.depression.com.au*

Depression Counselling and Psychologist Services in Australia

Even Keel *www.evenkeel.org.au*
> Bipolar Disorder Support Association

Depression Guide *www.depression-guide.com*
> A searchable index of articles and personal stories.

White Lion *www.whitelion.org.au*
> The White Lion Program promotes a range of initiatives for
> young people involved in or at risk of becoming involved in
> the youth justice system.

E-health

Reach Out! *www.reachout.com.au*

Somazone *www.somazone.com.au*

Climate.tv interactive *www.climate.tv*
> A self-management system for people with depression and anxiety.

MoodGYM *www.moodgym.anu.edu.au*
> Helps people identify problem emotions and develop skills
> for preventing and managing depression.

Ecouch *www.ecouch.anu.edu.au*
> Interactive online treatment program for people with panic
> disorder, including details of how to get involved in a new study.

Family and Friends

Carers Australia *www.carersaustralia.com.au*

It's All Right *www.itsallright.org*
   Support for young people who have a friend or family
   member with mental illness.

COMIC (Children of Mentally Ill Consumers)
   www.howstat.com/comic/contactus.asp
   A group of people who have parents with a mental illness.
   The website has resources and information on support
   groups.

ARAFMI (Association for Relatives and Friends of the
   Mentally Ill)
   Qld: *www.arafmiqld.org*
   NSW: *www.arafmi.org*
   SA: *www.depressionet.com.au/arafmi/arafmi-south-australia.html*
   Tas: *www.arafmitas.org.au*
   Vic: *www.arafemi.org.au*
   WA: *www.arafmi.asn.au*

Bullying and Online Harassment

Bullying No Way! *www.bullyingnoway.com.au*

NSW Police Force *www.police.nsw.gov.au*

Cybersmart Kids *www.cybersmartkids.com.au*

NetAlert *www.netalert.gov.au*

NetSmartz Workshop *www.netsmartz.org*

GetNetWise *www.getnetwise.org*

Netsafe *www.netsafe.org.nz*

Substance Abuse-related Disorders

Australian Drug Foundation *www.adf.org.au*

Alcohol and Other Drugs Council of Australia *www.adca.org.au*

Turning Point Alcohol & Drug Centre *www.turningpoint.org.au*
Information about substance use-related disorders and their management and an online interactive counselling service.

The National Drug & Alcohol Research Centre (NDARC) *www.ndarc.med.unsw.edu.au*
Information about substance use-related disorders and their management.

Family Drug Help *www.familydrughelp.sharc.org.au*
Family-focused information about substance use-related disorders and their management.

Drug Info Clearinghouse *www.druginfo.adf.org.au*
A searchable online library with drug and alcohol-related information.

Anorexia/Bulimia Nervosa

The Butterfly Foundation *www.thebutterflyfoundation.org.au*
Eating Disorders Foundation (in each state) *www.edf.org.au*
(links to state sites)

Endnotes

Chapter 3

1. Lynne Michael Blum's quote comes from the John Hopkins, Bloomberg School of Public Health Military Child Initiative 'Building Resilient Kids' website at *ww.jhsph.edu/mci*

Chapter 11

1. Many of the examples in this section are drawn from a training program for GPs and psychologists developed by the Centre for Developmental Psychiatry and Psychology at Monash University.

Other references used in this section are:

Clarke, G.N., Lewinsohn, P.M. and Hops, H., *Adolescent Coping with Depression Course: Leader's manual for adolescent groups*, Castalia Publishing Company, Eugene OR, 1990

Clarke, G.N., Lewinsohn, P.M. and Hops, H., *Adolescent Coping with Depression Course: Student workbook*, Castalia Publishing Company, Eugene OR, 1990

Graham, P. (ed.), *Cognitive Behavioural Therapy for Children and Families*, 2nd edn, Cambridge University Press, 2005

Treatment Protocol Project, *Management of Mental Disorders*, 4th edn, World Health Organization Collaborating Centre for Evidence in Mental Health Policy, Sydney, 2004

Bibliography

Eckersley, R., *Well and Good: Happiness, morality and meaning*, Cambridge University Press, Cambridge, 2001

Fuller, A., *Raising Real People: Creating a resilient family*, ACER Press, Melbourne, 2000

Kessler, R., *The Soul of Education: Helping students find a connection, compassion and character at school*, ASCD, Baltimore, 2000

Mackay, H., *Advance Australia . . . Where?*, Hachette Australia, Sydney, 2007

Mogel, W., *The Blessing of a Skinned Knee*, Penguin Putnam, New York, 2001

Shandler, S., *Ophelia Speaks: Adolescent girls write about their search for self*, HarperCollins, New York, 1999

Other resources

- Hickie, I. *Depression: Out of the Shadows: A guide to understanding depression and its treatment*. Produced in cooperation with *beyondblue: the national depression initiative* as part of the Australian Women's Weekly Health Series.
- Wigney, T., Eyers, K. and Parker, G. (eds) 2007, *Journeys with the Black Dog: Inspirational stories of bringing depression to heel*, Allen & Unwin, Sydney. Personal stories of living with depression—from first symptoms, getting diagnosed to recovery and management.
- Australian Post-traumatic Stress Disorder Guidelines for health professionals, produced by the Australian Centre for Post-traumatic Mental Health. The Guidelines are available to print at *www.acpmh.unimelb.edu.au*
- SPHERE Depression Management Program booklet. Visit *www.spheregp.com.au* for more information.
- SPHERE Structured Problem Solving and Cognitive Therapy for Depression booklet. Visit *www.spheregp.com.au* for more information.
- A brief guide to depression management. Visit *www.spheregp.com.au* for more information.
- The National Action Plan for Depression. Visit *www.health.gov.au/internet/main/Publishing.nsf/content/mental-pubs-n-depress* for a copy of this report.
- The National Mental Health Plan. Visit *www.mmha.org.au/information.policy/national-mental-health-plan*-2003-2008*.pdf* for a copy of this report.

- Guidelines to Responsible Reporting of Mental Health in the Media. Visit *www.mindframe-media.info* for more information.
- *Healthy Kids: A Parent's Guide*, produced by the Transcultural Mental Health Centre at The Children's Hospital at Westmead. This kit contains information on anorexia, anxiety, depression and disruptive disorders. It is available in nine languages: English, Arabic, Chinese, Vietnamese, Spanish, Turkish, Filipino, Hindi and Farsi.
- Multi-cultural Mental Health Australia *www.mmha.org.au* builds greater awareness of mental health and suicide prevention amongst Australians from culturally and linguistically diverse backgrounds.
- *Suicide Assessment & Intervention—Men at Risk*. An interactive CD-ROM that is empirically based. It outlines key risk factors for men and ways to identify warning signs. Through the use of realistic case studies, clinicians are given practical tips on conducting an assessment and responding to risk indicators. It includes a risk assessment guide that can be printed and used as an assessment tool. To find out more go to *www.menslineaus.org.au*
- *Grandparents Raising Grandchildren: An information resource for relative caregivers*. Visit *www.familiesandcommunities.sa. gov.au* or email gfgsainc@bigpond.com for a copy.
- JAM Distribution have developed a series of videos/DVDs that teach techniques for managing a range of mental health-related issues including depression, social phobia, panic and agoraphobia, bipolar disorder, schizophrenia and compulsive gambling. These techniques are taught in plain language by a range of psychologists, psychiatrists and consumers. You can purchase these resources by contacting jamdistribution@ hotmail.com

- Point Zero Youth Services *www.pointzero.org.au* Provides access to innovative 'prevention-based' programs that empower, support and educate young people and their communities in the Sydney metropolitan region.

Index

Notes

Notes

Notes

Notes

Notes

Notes

Notes

Notes

Save Your Life
& the lives of those you love
Your GP's 6-step guide to staying healthy longer

Professor Leanne Rowe and Professor Michael Kidd

Discover how to prevent or detect the 9 most common life-threatening illnesses and add years to your life.

What are your health risks? What early symptoms or signs should you really worry about? Are you concerned about a family member's health and how to motivate them to seek help?

You can take charge of your health with *Save Your Life*, a 6-step plan for staying healthy longer that contains all the latest scientific information on prevention and early detection of the 9 most common serious illnesses:

- heart disease
- stroke
- cancer
- lung disease
- depression
- dementia
- diabetes
- kidney disease
- osteoporosis.

THE ROYAL AUSTRALIAN COLLEGE OF GENERAL PRACTITIONERS

Endorsed by the Royal Australian College of General Practitioners

Written by two of Australia's best-known practising GPs and endorsed by the Royal Australian College of General Practitioners, *Save Your Life* is an essential reference for everyone who cares about their health or the health of someone they love.

Don't wait until you lose your health before it becomes important to you.